SYSTEMS, ORGANIZATIONS, ANALYSIS, MANAGEMENT:

a book of readings

McGRAW-HILL SERIES IN MANAGEMENT

Keith Davis, *Consulting Editor*

SYSTEMS, ORGANIZATIONS, ANALYSIS, MANAGEMENT:

A book of readings

DAVID I. CLELAND

Associate Professor
Industrial Engineering
Systems Management Engineering
   and Operations Research
School of Engineering
University of Pittsburgh

WILLIAM R. KING

Associate Professor
Graduate School of Business
University of Pittsburgh

McGRAW-HILL BOOK COMPANY

New York   St. Louis   San Francisco   Toronto
London   Sydney

SYSTEMS, ORGANIZATIONS, ANALYSIS, MANAGEMENT:
a book of readings

Library of Congress Catalog Card Number 68–54007

1 2 3 4 5 6 7 8 9 0   HDBP   7 5 4 3 2 1 0 6 9 8

PREFACE

The title chosen for this book of readings warrants immediate explanation to readers. The four unconnected words—systems, analysis, organizations, and management—are those which best describe the content of the book. It is a book about *systems* and the systems concept applied to *management* and *analysis* in *organizations*. Yet, in our initial discussions concerning a title, each proposed title which incorporated all of these salient aspects seemed tedious and verbose.

An indexing method used in the field of information retrieval provided the resolution of this dilemma. This method, KWIC (key-word-in-context), utilizes the key words of a title as a basis for indexing. Each index entry for a particular title consists of a key word followed by the remainder of the key words in the sequence in which they appear in the title. Thus, any title which we would have chosen using these four key words in the given order would have four index entries in a KWIC system:

systems, organizations, analysis, management
organizations, analysis, management, systems
analysis, management, systems, organizations
management, systems, organizations, analysis

The chosen title is the first of these index entries. It provides the same information about the content of the book which would be provided by an index entry. Hopefully, this will lead to better communication and an avoidance of the problems inherent in the grandiose titles often selected for readings books.

We were led to develop this set of readings after our perception of the inadequacies of most management texts resulted in a book entitled *Systems Analysis and Project Management*. In preparing that text, we drew on the work and thoughts of many of our colleagues both within and outside the field of management. With this task completed, it was suggested that a book of readings developed along similar modern lines would be valuable in several ways. First, it would be an invaluable complement to the basic book in that it would present the views of others in their own words and serve to better demonstrate the biases and personal values inherent in any good book. Moreover, it would permit a wider coverage of applications and ramifications of the systems concepts to which we focus attention.

However, one of the great utilities envisioned for a modern systems-oriented readings book is as *a complement to basic management texts which do not emphasize systems ideas.* We recognize that the treatment of some aspects of management thought and theory in systems-oriented texts such as ours is not as comprehensive as it is elsewhere. In seeking to demonstrate the applicability of modern systems concepts to both the planning and execution functions of management, we necessarily tended to deemphasize many management principles which are not of central importance to this thesis. In doing so, we produced a book which will be too narrow for the tastes of some teachers. Other texts with which we are familiar have similar biases.

On the other hand, a cursory treatment of systems ideas such as is given in most basic management texts is insufficient for the modern manager and student of management. Thus, a valid role for a readings book such as this is as a complementary vehicle to a basic nonsystems text.

We also envision that this book will play a role in the more advanced study of those who are already well versed in basic management ideas and practice. Of course, we sincerely hope that such a value is found by both students and practitioners, for systems ideas will become even more important in everyone's management task in the future than they are today. Particularly, we hope that those managers and management-oriented technical people who did not study systems concepts as a part of their formal training will make use of the wealth of knowledge put forth by management thinkers here.

Our sincere thanks go to the contributors— who are the real authors of the book. In most cases, we present their work in its original published form. In others, revisions have been made to render previously published material more compatible with the form of presentation.

Our contribution to this volume is in the introductory section and the introductions to the other sections. There, we attempt to set the theme for the book and to integrate the various papers into a consistent whole. For any inconsistencies or omissions, we alone are responsible.

The other contribution which we offer was both arduous and rewarding. We spent many months in reviewing the literature of a variety of fields. The piles of journals and individual papers in our offices were the focal point of many derisory comments from our colleagues. But the learning and discussion which the process stimulated was valuable to us, and it enhanced the quality of the papers finally selected. We are quick to point out that any book is the product of the attitudes and prejudices of its editors and that our biases and prejudices may not be particularly worthy ones. It is nonetheless true that according to our consistent criterion of subjective value, the papers which appear here are the best of hundreds which were considered. Unless our values are completely misdirected, the authors should feel a measure of pride in that selection.

The book is an attempt to collect the thought of recognized authorities in various fields as they apply to the modern ideas of systems analysis and management. A cursory examination of the book may lead one to the conclusion that it represents a continuous attack on the "traditional school" of management. On the contrary, our objective has been to continue to build on, rather than tear down, the existing theory of management. The traditional views of management are just as basic to contemporary thought as algebra is important to the study of higher mathematics.

In Section 1, modern organizations are viewed in an overall framework. Emphasis is placed on the differences between organizations of today and yesterday, and attempts are made to predict the form of typical organizations of the future. Section 2 discusses basic systems concepts and applications.

In Sections 3 and 4, the planning function of management is analyzed in both business and governmental contexts. The latter section discusses the planning, programming, and budgeting cycle which has been instituted in the federal government.

Sections 5 and 6 deal with systems analysis —the application of systems concepts and scientific methods to the planning function of management.

Section 7 discusses the recent techniques of management that require the establishment of a management system having no functional or organizational constraints. This new concept of "interorganizational" management, called *project management,* emerged primarily from the needs of the Department of Defense and the National Aeronautics and Space Administration.

Section 8 deals with the question of evaluating organizational progress in the management process. The material examines the use of network analysis and the more traditional control techniques such as Gantt charts and other methods to measure the cost, schedule, and performance factors of organizational activities.

Section 9 introduces what promises to be a useful view of the management process—the charting of interorganizational relationships. The material in this section questions the use of the traditional organizational chart as a means of portraying the functioning of an organization and offers in addition thereto views of modern organizational patterns.

We wish to extend our thanks to Janet Wheeler, Betty Holt, and Pat Doorley Wagel who helped prepare the manuscript and performed many other kind acts of sympathy and assistance. We also wish to thank Lloyd Dunlap, Al Frey, and Jerry Zoffer for having contributed to environments which facilitated the accomplishment of our task. And, of course, we owe our greatest debt to the authors and copyright holders who kindly gave permission for us to use their material. Finally, our families, who are an intrinsic part of each of our undertakings, deserve at least a brief mention for their tolerance of their fathers.

DAVID I. CLELAND

WILLIAM R. KING

CONTENTS

INTRODUCTION

The modern organization—be it governmental, entrepreneurial, or ecclesiastical in nature—is undergoing radical changes in its basic structure, its method of operation, and its outlook on the world around it. This change is a revolutionary one, yet it is so unobtrusive that many people, even those who are a part of large organizations themselves, do not recognize that it is happening.

Since World War II, an ever-changing environment and the consequent changing responses to that environment have become the established patterns for most organizations. In effect, change has become a way of life.

The manifestations of change are apparent in the operations and makeup of virtually all large organizations. The organization's perception of its dynamic environment has resulted in conscious *planning for change,* in lieu of the established pattern of reacting to it. Moreover, new organizational forms have been developed to permit more flexible patterns of operation, so that in some of its salient features, the modern organization looks little like its pre-World War II predecessor.

Nowhere is the change which has taken place so apparent as in the organization's decision-making process. Formal *analysis* now plays an important role in decision making where once almost total emphasis was placed on executive judgment, experience, and intuition. The modern approach to decision making complements judgment with objective analysis built on a foundation of mathematics and statistics, thereby permitting a blending of the objective and subjective in a fashion which amplifies the executive's ability to cope with complex decision situations.

To understand the basic changes which are taking place, it is useful to begin by considering the organizational form which once was universal and is still pervasive—the *bureaucracy.*

BUREAUCRACY

The bureaucracy is characterized by a number of fixed jurisdictional areas, each with official duties and with individuals who have authority regarding the discharge of these duties. The "system" operates according to fixed rules of superior and subordinate. Individuals are appointed to official positions by superiors, and their status with respect to subordinates is guaranteed by rules of rank.

Bureaucracy has been the basic pattern of organization found in the traditional model of management. Although the bureaucratic form is usually associated with government organizations, the structure and processes of bureaucracy are found in many contemporary industrial organizations.

The bureaucracy's primary advantages have been argued by Max Weber.

> Bureaucratization offers above all the optimum possibility for carrying through the principle of specializing administrative functions according to purely objective considerations. Individual performances are allocated to functionaries who have specialized training and who by constant practice learn more and more. The "objective" discharge of business primarily means a discharge of business according to *calculable rules* and without regard for persons.[1]

Weber's phrase "without regard for persons" is of central importance to the bureaucratic concept, for the roots of the bureaucracy lie in basic assumptions about people and the way in which they are motivated.

The bureaucratic view is that the "passions'" of humans must be strictly controlled by the organization in order to effectively direct their energies toward the accomplishment of the goals of the organization. The motivation of people under bureaucracy theoretically rested principally on economic matters. Frederick Taylor, "the father of scientific management," concentrated his attention on improving the efficiency of the individual in the work situation, to the detriment of the human relations aspect of management. Keith Davis summarizes Taylor's attitude towards the human element by stating: "To Taylor and his contemporaries, human problems stood in the way of production, and so should be removed."[2]

Advocates of the bureaucratic form of organization justified the organizational form and the management techniques in terms of the "principles" of management theory. The principles were often based on a complex of assumptions about organizational goals and processes, often unstated, and lacking empirical validation.

The concept of authority offers a good illustration. Authority is defined by the bureaucracy as the legal power to act. According to the bureaucratic tradition, goals are achieved by making them the explicit responsibility of some executive. Then, if that official is given sufficient legal authority (through a form of documented job description, organizational charter, etc.) and the necessary resources, the goal can be reached, regardless of its complexity. Once the executive determines the direction his organization will take, the process of the day-to-day accomplishment of the objectives becomes a matter of organizational routine. The significance of peer-to-peer and technician-to-generalist relations are neglected.

Of course, it is just not that simple. Rigid authority patterns do not assure the accomplishment of goals. In fact, it has been vividly illustrated that the inflexibility of the bureaucratic system may well not even be a good way of assuring a high *likelihood* of achieving goals. People are indeed important, and their motivations must be accounted for if goals are to be accomplished efficiently.

Perhaps the most incriminating assumption of the bureaucratic model concerns the verticality of the organizational form. When compared to the actual flow of work and organizational deliberations, many of the assumptions surrounding the principles seem to be based on a theoretical model of an organization which does not, in reality, exist. Modern organizations are taking on many different forms, thus testing the bureaucratic model of management which emphasizes the vertical flow of authority and responsibility. Structure in these modern organizations is being subordinated in favor of *processes* or *flows* of resources and relationships necessary to sustain the organization in its competitive environment.

Two primary conceptual developments have contributed to the evolution of modern organizations along nonbureaucratic lines. The first of these developments is the *systems concept,* and the second is the growing awareness of the significance of the organization's *human subsystem.*

---

[1] *Max Weber,* Essays in Sociology, *edited and translated by H. H. Gerth and C. Wright Mills, Oxford University Press, Fair Lawn, N.J., 1946.*
[2] *Keith Davis,* Human Relations at Work, *McGraw-Hill Book Company, New York, 1967, p. 9.*

THE SYSTEMS CONCEPT

Much has been written and said about the "systems concept" or "systems approach" in organizational thought. Much of this, particularly that said in the context of computer-oriented systems, is cloaked in an aura of mystery and sophistication which is unwarranted. The systems approach is neither new nor sophisticated. Neither is it necessarily related to the quantitative analyses which have made such great use of it.

It would indeed be presumptuous to credit the current generation of academicians and practitioners with the development of the systems concept in management. Although certain contemporaries have made significant contributions in integrating and conceptualizing the systems view,[3] the germ of the idea appeared as early as 1912.[4] Indeed, the use of the concept certainly precedes the use of the word "systems" to describe it.

A system may be defined in dictionary terms as "an organized or complex whole; an assemblage or combination of things or parts forming a complex or unitary whole." Thus, virtually everything is a system. The obvious contexts in which the layman uses the term, e.g., the Mississippi River system, the nervous system, etc., are appropriate to the definition. So, too, the universe is a system and so, too, is every organization a system.

In elementary terms, the systems approach may be thought of as requiring that the manager and analyst *adopt a view of as large a system as is practical*. Carried to the extreme, this says that each manager and analyst should consider their role and the implications of their actions on the universe. The obvious constraint, however, is the phrase "as is practical."

Thus, the systems approach in organizations is the antithesis of the bureaucracy with its neatly defined areas of endeavor and communications through the chain of command. The systems view presumes that interactions at all levels are analyzed and used to the advantage of the total system. Moreover, implicit in the systems approach is a deemphasis of the parochial goals of functional units and a corresponding emphasis on total system performance.

Even management functions themselves have an interrelatedness and thus may be visualized as a system. Planning and organization precede control; yet to control we must have a standard against which to compare results and, when necessary, to correct performance. Development of corporate strategy in the planning process precedes the execution of that strategy; the development of strategy can do little for the organization if there is not a clear understanding as to where the responsibility rests for the execution of the strategy. Of course, the carrying out of the strategy requires different skills. Whereas the development of strategy requires analytical and abstract skills, the execution of the strategy requires administrative and "human" skills. Thus we see the interdependencies that exist in the management process when a parochial view, say in planning, can reduce and even endanger the efficacy of the total management system.

Product Systems

Some illustrations of the systems approach will serve to put the idea into focus. What, for instance, is the systems view of a company's product? The answer to this may be attained by asking about objectives—both the company's and the potential consumer's. If a cosmetics manufacturer thinks of his product objective as "selling face powder" and that of his customer as "buying face powder," he is not taking a systems view. The customer's desire is to buy *beauty* and the skillful manufacturer will therefore make it his objective to sell beauty. Obviously, face powder may be one phase of this, but it is not everything, and in fact, in the context of the views of others toward "beauty," it may play no role at all. Thus, the systems approach to marketing involves a recognition of the basic objectives of the consumer and plans for ways to fulfill those objectives. The skillful marketing system analyst will plan a *product system*, e.g., a complex of interrelated products and lines associated with beauty rather than one product or several unrelated products.

A simple illustration of a product system is the one whose elements are *color-coordinated* bedspreads, draperies and curtains, towels, etc.

[3] *See Richard A. Johnson et al.,* The Theory and Management of Systems, *McGraw-Hill Book Company, New York, 1967.*

[4] *See Henry P. Kendall,* Scientific Management: First Conference at the Amos Tuck School, Dartmouth College, *The Plimpton Press, Norwood, Massachusetts, 1912, p. 13.*

By relating the elements one to the other via their complementary function *and* their esthetic appeal, the marketing planner creates a system and takes advantage of the relationships among the elements of the system to increase total sales.

Organizational Systems

The systems approach to organization involves a view of as large a system as feasible in terms of its components and their relationships. In directing and operating an *organizational system,* the manager is faced with a desire for *overall effectiveness* coupled with conflicting *organizational goals.* Thus, each of the functional units of a large company has its own parochial goals, which may well be incompatible with one another. Perhaps the production department wishes to manufacture large quantities of few items in order to reduce costly machine setups and idle time, whereas the sales force desires inventories of a wide variety of items so that any order can be rapidly filled.

So, too, are there conflicting overall objectives of organizations. For example, a desire for profit and a desire for a satisfied work force are not always compatible since, at the superficial level at least, higher wages presumably contribute to lower profits and greater employee satisfaction.

In applying the systems view of an organization, one studies the constituent elements, e.g., the functional units, *and their relationships* and seeks to integrate them in a fashion which contributes to *overall goals.* (Of course, these overall goals are themselves potentially incompatible, so that some resolution of them must first be made.) Consequently, some functional units within an organization may not achieve their parochial objectives, for what is best for the whole is not necessarily best for each component of the system. Thus, when a wide variety of products are produced in relatively small quantities, the apparent performance of the production department may suffer. Yet, if this leads to greater total revenues because no sales are lost, the overall result may be positive. This simple realization is the essence of the systems viewpoint. Its acceptance and utilization has led many organizations to more effective management decisions and to organizing for the efficient execution of those decisions.

The basic difference between the bureaucratic view and the systems view is the difference between *structure* and *process.* The bureaucracy is a hierarchial structure. The systems view of the organization is one involving a set of *flows,* e.g., of information, people, material, money, and a "stream of projects," that represent the work which the organization performs.

Organizational Subsystems

Constituent elements of a total organization may themselves be viewed as systems. For example, the production subsystem is a system which is itself made up of people, machines, flows of products, flows of information, etc. There is also a marketing and financial subsystem within every business organization. Throughout these realizations of the systems concept lies the recognition that technological and social changes have made our economic and social institutions so complex and interdependent that the interactions among their parts and activities warrant as much attention as do their separate functions. This formal interaction between the parts of a system becomes the basis for the conceptual framework of the systems approach.

Other elements of the organization which cut across functional lines may also be viewed in the systems context. For instance, one may view the management information system of a company—that collection of reports, surveys, and other information which is collected and processed to provide a basis for decision making. The management information system, of course, also includes the people, data-processing equipment, models, etc., which contribute to the flow of information.

Applications of Systems Concepts

The systems concept and the modern ideas of human relations have reached fruition in changing organizations in two major areas of organizational management—planning and execution. The planning or *decision-making* aspect of organizations has been influenced by the systems approach through the application of *systems analysis.* In the execution phase of management, *systems (project) management* has been the focal point for the application of systems concepts.

Systems and planning. One of the major changes which has occurred in organizational management in the past decade is the increasing emphasis on long-range planning. In a dynamic environment such as that in which most modern organizations function, it is necessary to do more than to react to changes in the environment. Long-range planning as a formal activity within an organization reflects the need for organizations to influence the future and to take advantage of the opportunities which it presents. That such opportunities will be available is self-evident. To plan for them requires an answer to the question: "What business should we be in?"

Planning for change requires viewing the company in the context of the greater system of which it is a part and in estimating future opportunity in terms of present-day decisions. Planning serves as the focus of organizational effort in assessing risk and uncertainty in the future. The proper pursuit of planning requires a flexible organization, particularly in terms of the attitudes and skills of the key executives. An organizational structure that is suitable for one product or market may not be suitable for others. Innovation in all the functional areas of a business can enable the organization to develop a system of plans which will influence its environment; the organization will not merely be responding to what it sees its competitors doing. If the organizational philosophy is based on the main tenets of bureaucracy, with its preoccupation of organizational verticality and fixed personal roles, then adherence to the existing order of affairs can be expected. If, on the other hand, the organizational executives do not want to tacitly accept their fate in the ensuing environment, the organization can influence its future.

In this respect, Dr. Fred Polak developed a theory that the future of a civilization, a country, or a people is determined in large measure by its "images of the future." He contends that it is possible to measure these images of the future, and it may be possible to alter or adjust them, thus guiding a nation's or people's future. According to Polak, if a society has optimistic ideas, dynamic aspirations, and cohesive ambitions, the civilization will grow and prosper. If it exhibits negative trends, uncertain ideals, and hesitant faith, the society is in danger of disintegrating. The idea again is that by thinking about the future, man creates that future according to his image.

The application of these ideas to business follow naturally according to Polak. Indeed, history shows that most great industrial enterprises have grown on the strength of an image of the future held consciously or subconsciously by their leaders.[5]

One of the more dramatic aspects of modern business planning is found in the changing executives' attitudes toward corporate objectives and strategy. Today's corporation faces rapidly changing environmental conditions coupled with intensive competition. The need for the formulation of an explicit corporate strategy has never been more acute. The business firm faces groups of "claimants," each seeking satisfaction of a particular claim. To say that the stockholder's claim of profit is superior to the claim of a customer who seeks the service of a product is to take a position inconsistent with today's social environment. From whose viewpoint should the corporate strategy be developed? The traditional view of a corporation would emphasize the common stockholder. On the other hand, one of the aims of capitalism is to encourage wide distribution of the benefits of political freedom and private property; thus, the claim of creditors, employees, customers, governments, and competitors, to name a few, must be factored into the development of the corporate strategy.

Long-range strategic planning and the systems concept are interrelated through *systems analysis*—the formal analysis of the strategic decisions of the organization. All organizations face a scarcity of resources; there is never enough of the resources required to do everything to the degree which one would like to do it. Thus, money allocated to product development is unavailable for advertising, and salesmen assigned to promote Product A are unavailable for promotion of Product B. The scarcity of resources implies a choice between alternatives, and complex choice situations involving great uncertainties are best handled through a combination of formal analysis and subjective judgment.

The reason for this is pragmatic rather than conceptual. The human mind is quite capable of performing analysis. Hence, it is possible that an individual could apply the systems con-

[5] *Weldon B. Gibson, as cited in* "Guideposts for Forward Planning," Long-Range Planning for Management, *edited by David W. Ewing, Harper and Row, Publishers, Incorporated, New York, 1958, pp. 488–489.*

cept and perform a total systems analysis on a totally subjective basis. However, it is unlikely that anyone could actually do so in any but the most elemental variety of system. The human mind, as presently developed, can comprehend only so much at one time, and the application of the systems concept in decision analysis requires that many complexities and interrelationships between problem elements be considered. Even if the manager were able to reduce the complexities to manageable proportions by abstracting out all but the salient aspects, he has no guarantee that he can subjectively relate them in a fashion which is either logical or consistent.

Systems analysis is a combination of a set of tools, philosophies, and techniques which is designed to facilitate choices between alternatives in a fashion which maximizes the effectiveness of resources available to the organization. Basic to the analysis is the flow of information available to the firm. This information takes the form of intelligence about costs and the effectiveness of different ways of meeting organizational objectives. The information, both qualitative and quantitative, when properly developed and used by the decision maker, can provide a potent force in ensuring that the total volume of resources is effectively allocated to achieve organizational objectives.

The fields called *operations research, management science*, and *systems analysis* are those whose scopes encompass the application of objective scientific methods to the solution of management decision problems. Practitioners in each of these fields may rely on models—formal abstractions of real-world systems—to predict the outcomes of the various available alternatives in complex decision problems.

Because these models are usually symbolic, it is possible to reduce complex relationships to paper and, using techniques of logic and mathematics, to consider interrelationships and combinations of circumstances which would be beyond the scope of any human. Models permit experimentation of a kind which is unavailable in many environments; one may experiment on the model which describes a system without experimenting on the system itself.

Of course, this does not mean that the decision maker cedes his responsibility for making decisions to some mystical scientific process or that his judgment and intuition do not play a major role in decision making. By

the nature of the mathematics which are available, models have one of the same "deficiencies" as does the human brain in that they are able to consider only a part of the real-world decision problem. Other parts are omitted either as being relatively unimportant, or because they cannot be handled using existing techniques. The difference between explicit models and subjective decision analysis using nebulous "models" which exist in the mind of the manager is one of degree. The *process* is very similar, but explicit models formalize salient characteristics and relationships which may be blurred in the mind of a man. Explicit consideration is given to those aspects of the real-world situation which should be included in the model and those which should be abstracted out. Men tend to include in their "mental models" the first (or last) aspects which occur to them and to exclude others which stretch the bounds of their comprehension. Moreover, once the explicit model has been constructed, the objective approach has the guarantee of logic and consistency, which is not usually a feature of the application of judgment and intuition in problem-solving.

The role of the manager's judgment and intuition is merely refocused by the systems approach. It is directed toward those aspects of problems which are best handled subjectively. The use of systems analysis provides insights into the problem in that it focuses attention on the important variables and identifies the areas where subjective judgment is required. The analysis clearly states the areas where judgments have been utilized and leaves them to be challenged and defended as necessary. This permits calm, expert judgment on each specific aspect, rather than gross judgments encompassing factors related to wide varieties of disciplines and areas of experience. The best illustration of this value of scientific problem analysis involves the *evaluative* and *predictive* judgments which are a part of most complex problems. The objective approach clearly separates those judgments related to *the worth of a state of affairs* (evaluative) and those related to *the future course of events* (predictive). In the mind of a decision maker, such judgments often become indistinguishable. For example, the executive concerned with a new product decision problem must necessarily predict the sales level to be anticipated and the worth of that sales level. The predictive aspect is independent of the organization's goals, whereas the evaluative one intrinsically depends on them. If both aspects are considered simultaneously, the executive is likely to become confused and achieve poorer results than he might if the two aspects were treated separately.

Another aspect of the refocusing of the manager's judgment through scientific analysis is that this approach involves utilizing judgment in integrating the results of objective analysis with the predicted effect of unconsidered problem elements, and arriving at a decision based on the totality of available information. In effect, the systems approach to planning may be viewed as a logically consistent method of reducing a large part of a complex problem to a simple output which can be used by the decision maker in conjunction with considerations, in arriving at a "best" decision. It permits him to focus his attention on the aspects of the problem which are most deserving and to restrict the attention which he allocates to those things which are best handled more formally. Such an integration of science and intuition permits consideration of the interrelationships of functional activities. In simple terms, it enables the manager to get the "big picture" in its proper perspective, rather than requiring (or permitting) him to devote attention to relatively minor aspects of the total system.

Systems and execution.   The systems concept has not only caused great changes in the planning or strategic decision-making portion of the manager's function, but has also caused revolutionary changes in the fashion in which decisions are executed. The most striking example of this is the emergence of *project management*. Today certain aerospace companies use project-management techniques in their commercial airplane divisions, and large chemical companies use project methods of management in their R&D activities.

The use of project techniques grew out of the need for a management philosophy to cope with the increasing complexity of product-development activities. Engineering-development contracts have generally increased in scope and have a better-defined beginning and end and more specificity of cost, schedule, and/or technology (performance). The pace of competition in product development requires large capital investment with increased risks

in timing of the product. The organizational arrangement necessary to focus management attention on an *ad hoc* project takes many forms; it essentially consists of *integral teams superimposed on the vertical structure of the organization*. The purpose of these teams is to provide a focal point for pulling together all functional aspects of the project. Yet there is another purpose, albeit subtle, of establishing such teams as a means of providing recognition, security, and a sense of contribution to the members of the unit whose individual efforts might otherwise be lost in the morass of functional bureaucracy.

In today's economy, any going concern is constantly confronted with a "stream of projects" that supplies the work for the members of the organization. Each project is in a different stage of completion; one may be merely a concept undergoing feasibility study, another in development, some in production, and some in the process of being phased out of the product line in favor of newer models. The application of systems ideas to this stream of projects, each with its own problems and peculiarities, implies that an individual be designated as Project Manager, with the responsibility for keeping abreast of all the company's work on that project. Project management, therefore, is a general management activity and includes such functions as planning, organizing, motivating, integrating, directing, and controlling efforts to obtain a specific goal. In many ways, project management is similar to functional or traditional management. The project manager, however, may have to accomplish his ends through the efforts of individuals who are paid and promoted by someone else in the chain of command.

The pacing factor in acquiring a new plant, in building a bridge, or in developing a new product is often not technology but management. The technology to accomplish an *ad hoc* project may be in hand but cannot be put to proper use because the approach to the management is inadequate and unrealistic. Too often this failure can be attributed to an attempt to fit the project to an existing management organization rather than *molding the management to fit the needs of the project*. The project manager, therefore, is somewhat of a maverick in the business world. No set pattern exists by which he can operate. His philosophy of management may depart radically from traditional theory. He may use established principles, but he uses them merely as guides to his thinking, for his way of operating may depart radically from the traditional. Furthermore, his task is finite in duration; when he accomplishes the project objectives, he no longer has a function, but must return to his functional organization or be assigned to manage an oncoming project. He is, in effect, constantly working himself out of a job.

The project manager's position is based on the realization that modern organizations are so complex as to preclude effective management using only traditional organizational structure and relationships. Top management cannot be expected to comprehend all of the details and intricacies involved in the management of each activity, be they weapons systems which are under development, products being marketed, or clients being serviced. Functional units properly give greater concern to their function than they do to individual products or projects. Thus, the need for a manager who can cut across traditional functional lines to bring together the resources required to achieve *project goals* is clear.

Just as the systems viewpoint necessitates consideration of the combined effect and interrelationships of various organizational functions in the manager's planning task, so, too, does it require integration of these functions at the execution level. The project manager is able to operate through the various functional managers in directing the resources which are necessary to the effective pursuance of a project. He is thereby able to focus his attention on *project goals* rather than on parochial production, marketing, or financial goals. As such, he serves as the instrument for implementing decisions in terms of the same structure in which they are made—the system.

THE HUMAN SUBSYSTEM

There is one universal resource found in all organizations—the human element; there are no "peopleless" organizations. Yet if one examines the traditional organizational chart as typical of the reality of organization form, he would reasonably assume that organizations are devoid of the human element. This is so because the pyramidal chart fails to display an adequate abstraction of the true interrelationships of people in their day-to-day activities.

We still depend on the hierarchial model of management as a basis for our organizational models—and in so doing continue to portray the vertical order of affairs and neglect the collateral relationships that make up the work-a-day business world.

In bureaucracy the human resource is viewed as an objective element whose rewards and punishments are based on a standard model of man motivated solely by economic factors and lacking ambition and a sense of responsibility.[6] The human element is looked upon as something which must be controlled via a system of rules, procedures, prescribed roles, and prescribed authority.

The modern view of the human element is vastly different from this view; the multi-dimensional nature of human motivation is well-recognized and accepted. Individuals are motivated for many reasons besides economic rewards. Social and psychological motivations are important as well. The group in which the individual works is of critical importance to the satisfaction of his desires, for these satisfactions are in the form of self-fulfillment, self-esteem, and the approval and acceptance of the social group. Today's accepted value systems recognize the need for the industrial organization to assume more social responsibility as well as to contribute to the economic well-being of the individual. The values resulting from such a view include the integration of the needs of the individual with the needs of the social group to which he belongs. In turn, by meeting individual needs in terms of human dignity, recognition, and self-actualization, the needs of the organization can be better met.

The increased recognition of the value of the human subsystem as it complements the technical one portends more complexity in the manager's job. This, together with the development of information systems which follow no lines on the organizational chart and the growing interdependence of social and economic relationships, are drastically changing the situation which the manager must face. The pace of technology has made many of our "tried-and-tested" management and organization theories obsolete. In order to survive, the business must prepare to adapt to these changes.

[6] *Fortunately this view has been successfully challenged. One of the best challenges is found in Douglas McGregor,* The Human Side of Enterprise, *McGraw-Hill Book Company, New York, 1960.*

SECTION 1

Modern Organizations

Change has become a way of life in modern organizations. The people who manage these organizations are discovering that the traditional methods of planning and executing decisions, and indeed, the day-to-day organization and operating procedures of the enterprise, were not designed to function in such a climate.

The manager's perception of this dynamic environment has led to the institution of radical changes in organizations to enable them to effectively deal with these changes. These changes have centered around a departure from the traditional vertical structure of organization and have strengthened the role of peer-to-peer relationships that earlier management theory relegated to the "informal" organization. Organizational patterns have emerged which are multidimensional in nature as reflected by the "matrix" form.

The concept of a matrix organization evolves from the imposition of a "stream of projects" on the functionally aligned organization. Of course, "projects" are performed by all organizations whatever their structure may be. For example, the building of a new plant or the development of a new product each may be thought of as a project. However, a project may involve much more elementary activities, such as the gathering of information to complete a questionnaire which an industry association requests. If such a questionnaire must be partially completed by a number of functionaries and departments, it must flow through the organization in much the same fashion as do products, information, etc. This then is the essence of the matrix organization—a stream of ad hoc activities superimposed on the traditional functional organization.

Product management *is a marketing term used to describe an organizational pattern which is analogous to the matrix organization. The product manager is vested with responsibility for a given product or brand. At the extreme, he handles all phases of the marketing of a product—pricing, market research, advertising, promotion, etc. He does this in a fashion similar to the way he would operate his own business, and he is responsible for integrating and coordinating the activities of the functional departments which are concerned with the product.*

The concept of project *management, as it was initially employed in the development of weapons systems, and that of* product *management, which relates primarily to the* execution *of marketing plans for a product, can be effectively combined in an organization. For example, a project may be established to bring a product idea to marketing fruition. At that point, the life cycle of the project changes and a product manager assumes responsibility for marketing the product. Of course, some of the people may be involved in product management as well as in the project phase. However, many specialists whose talents are needed at one stage of development will not be needed at another, and almost certainly the same specialists will not be needed to execute marketing plans as were needed to develop the product.*

One way of viewing this relationship between project management and product management is in the composition of the project team. As different skills become necessary, the project's complement changes until, as fullscale marketing is embarked upon, most of the original people will no longer be involved. Usually, the project responsibility also transfers at this point from the project leader *to a* product manager.

In this Section, a series of papers which question the traditional model of organizations is followed by an introduction to some of the modern ideas of organizational structure—the "matrix" organization and product management. In the concluding paper, Max Ways considers both the changes which have occurred in today's organizations and the trends which will determine the future structure and operating methods of those enterprises.

READING 1

THE COMING DEATH OF BUREAUCRACY*

Warren G. Bennis

Not far from the new Government Center in downtown Boston, a foreign visitor walked up to a sailor and asked why American ships were built to last only a short time. According to the tourist, "The sailor answered without hesitation that the art of navigation is making such rapid progress that the finest ship would become obsolete if it lasted beyond a few years." In these words which fell accidentally from an uneducated man, I began to recognize the general and systematic idea upon which your great people direct all their concerns."

The foreign visitor was that shrewd observer of American morals and manners, Alexis de Tocqueville, and the year was 1835. He would not recognize Scollay Square today. But he had caught the central theme of our country: its preoccupation, its *obsession* with change. One thing is, however, new since de Tocqueville's time: the *acceleration* of newness, the changing

* *Reprinted by permission from* Think *Magazine, published by IBM, copyright 1966 by International Business Machines Corporation.*

scale and scope of change itself. As Dr. Robert Oppenheimer said, ". . . the world alters as we walk in it, so that the years of man's life measure not some small growth or rearrangement or moderation of what was learned in childhood, but a great upheaval."

How will these accelerating changes in our society influence human organizations?

A short while ago, I predicted that we would, in the next 25 to 50 years, participate in the end of bureaucracy as we know it and in the rise of new social systems better suited to the 20th-century demands of industrialization. This forecast was based on the evolutionary principle that every age develops an organizational form appropriate to its genius, and that the prevailing form, known by sociologists as bureaucracy and by most businessmen as "damn bureaucracy," was out of joint with contemporary realities. I realize now that my distant prophecy is already a distinct reality so that prediction is already foreshadowed by practice.

I should like to make clear that by bureaucracy I mean a chain of command structured on the lines of a pyramid—the typical structure which coordinates the business of almost every human organization we know of: industrial, governmental, of universities and research and development laboratories, military, religious, voluntary. I do *not* have in mind those fantasies so often dreamed up to describe complex organizations. These fantasies can be summarized in two grotesque stereotypes. The first I call "Organization as Inkblot"—an actor steals around an uncharted wasteland, growing more restive and paranoid by the hour, while he awaits orders that never come. The other specter is "Organization as Big Daddy"—the actors are square people plugged into square holes by some omniscient and omnipotent genius who can cradle in his arms the entire destiny of man by way of computer and TV. Whatever the first image owes to Kafka, the second owes to George Orwell's *Nineteen Eighty-four*.

Bureaucracy, as I refer to it here, is a useful social invention that was perfected during the industrial revolution to organize and direct the activities of a business firm. Most students of organizations would say that its anatomy consists of the following components:

A well-defined chain of command.
A system of procedures and rules for dealing with all contingencies relating to work activities.
A division of labor based on specialization.
Promotion and selection based on technical competence.
Impersonality in human relations.

It is the pyramid arrangement we see on most organizational charts.

The bureaucratic "machine model" was developed as a reaction against the personal subjugation, nepotism and cruelty, and the capricious and subjective judgments which passed for managerial practices during the early days of the industrial revolution. Bureaucracy emerged out of the organizations' need for order and precision and the workers' demands for impartial treatment. It was an organization ideally suited to the values and demands of the Victorian era. And just as bureaucracy emerged as a creative response to a radically new age, so today new organizational shapes are surfacing before our eyes.

First I shall try to show why the conditions of our modern industrialized world will bring about the death of bureaucracy. In the second part of this article I will suggest a rough model of the organization of the future.

There are at least four relevant threats to bureaucracy:

1 Rapid and unexpected change.
2 Growth in size where the volume of an organization's traditional activities is not enough to sustain growth. (A number of factors are included here, among them: bureaucratic overhead; tighter controls and impersonality due to bureaucratic sprawls; outmoded rules and organizational structures.)
3 Complexity of modern technology where integration between activities and persons of very diverse, highly specialized competence is required.
4 A basically psychological threat springing from a change in managerial behavior.

It might be useful to examine the extent to which these conditions exist *right now:*

1 *Rapid and unexpected change*—Bureaucracy's strength is its capacity to efficiently manage the routine and predictable in human affairs. It is almost enough to cite the knowledge and population explosion to raise doubts about its contemporary viability. More revealing, however, are the statistics which demonstrate these overworked phrases:

Our productivity output per man hour may now be doubling almost every 20 years rather than every 40 years, as it did before World War II.
The Federal Government alone spent $16 billion in research and development activities in 1965; it will spend $35 billion by 1980.
The time lag between a technical discovery and recognition of its commercial uses was: 30 years before World War I, 16 years between the Wars, and only 9 years since World War II.
In 1946, only 42 cities in the world had populations of more than one million. Today there are 90. In 1930, there were 40 people for each square mile of the earth's land surface. Today there are 63. By 2000, it is expected, the figure will have soared to 142.

Bureaucracy, with its nicely defined chain of command, its rules and its rigidities, is ill-adapted to the rapid change the environment now demands.

2 *Growth in size*—While, in theory, there may be no natural limit to the height of a

bureaucratic pyramid, in practice the element of complexity is almost invariably introduced with great size. International operation, to cite one significant new element, is the rule rather than exception for most of our biggest corporations. Firms like Standard Oil Company (New Jersey) with over 100 foreign affiliates, Mobil Oil Corporation, The National Cash Register Company, Singer Company, Burroughs Corporation and Colgate-Palmolive Company derive more than half their income or earnings from foreign sales. Many others—such as Eastman Kodak Company, Chas. Pfizer & Company, Inc., Caterpillar Tractor Company, International Harvester Company, Corn Products Company and Minnesota Mining & Manufacturing Company—make from 30 to 50 percent of their sales abroad. General Motors Corporation sales are not only nine times those of Volkswagen, they are also bigger than the Gross National Product of the Netherlands and well over the GNP of a hundred other countries. If we have seen the sun set on the British Empire, we may never see it set on the empires of General Motors, ITT, Shell and Unilever.

3 *Increasing diversity—Today's activities require persons of very diverse, highly specialized competence.*

Numerous dramatic examples can be drawn from studies of labor markets and job mobility. At some point during the past decade, the U.S. became the first nation in the world ever to employ more people in service occupations than in the production of tangible goods. Examples of this trend:

In the field of education, the *increase* in employment between 1950 and 1960 was greater than the total number employed in the steel, copper and aluminum industries.

In the field of health, the *increase* in employment between 1950 and 1960 was greater than the total number employed in automobile manufacturing in either year.

In financial firms, the *increase* in employment between 1950 and 1960 was greater than total employment in mining in 1960.

These changes, plus many more that are harder to demonstrate statistically, break down the old, industrial trend toward more and more people doing either simple or undifferentiated chores.

Hurried growth, rapid change and increase in specialization—pit these three factors against the five components of the pyramid structure described on page 12, and we should expect the pyramid of bureaucracy to begin crumbling.

4 *Change in managerial behavior*—There is, I believe, a subtle but perceptible change in the philosophy underlying management behavior. Its magnitude, nature and antecedents, however, are shadowy because of the difficulty of assigning numbers. (Whatever else statistics do for us, they most certainly provide a welcome illusion of certainty.) Nevertheless, real change seems under way because of:

a. A new concept of *man,* based on increased knowledge of his complex and shifting needs, which replaces an over-simplified, innocent, push-button idea of man.

b. A new concept of *power,* based on collaboration and reason, which replaces a model of power based on coercion and threat.

c. A new concept of *organizational values,* based on humanistic-democratic ideals, which replaces the depersonalized mechanistic value system of bureaucracy.

The primary cause of this shift in management philosophy stems not from the bookshelf but from the manager himself. Many of the behavioral scientists, like Douglas McGregor or Rensis Likert, have clarified and articulated —even legitimized—what managers have only half registered to themselves. I am convinced, for example, that the popularity of McGregor's book, *The Human Side of Enterprise,* was based on his rare empathy for a vast audience of managers who are wistful for an alternative to the mechanistic concept of authority, i.e., that he outlined a vivid utopia of more authentic human relationships than most organizational practices today allow. Furthermore, I suspect that the desire for relationships in business has little to do with a profit motive per se, though it is often rationalized as doing so. The real push for these changes stems from the need, not only to humanize the organization, but to use it as a crucible of personal growth and the development of self-realization.[1]

The core problems confronting any organiza-

[1] *Let me propose an hypothesis to explain this tendency. It rests on the assumption that man has a basic need for transcendental experiences, somewhat like the psychological rewards which William James claimed religion provided—"an assurance of safety and a temper of peace, and, in relation to others, a preponderance of loving affections." Can it be that as religion has become secularized, less transcendental, men search for substitutes such as close interpersonal relationships, psychoanalysis— even the release provided by drugs such as LSD?*

tion fall, I believe, into five major categories. First, let us consider the problems, then let us see how our 20th-century conditions of constant change have made the bureaucratic approach to these problems obsolete.

1 *Integration.* The problem is how to integrate individual needs and management goals. In other words, it is the inescapable conflict between individual needs (like "spending time with the family") and organizational demands (like meeting deadlines).

Under 20th-century conditions of constant change there has been an emergence of human sciences and a deeper understanding of man's complexity. Today, integration encompasses the entire range of issues concerned with incentives, rewards and motivations of the individual, and how the organization succeeds or fails in adjusting to these issues. In our society, where personal attachments play an important role, the individual is appreciated, and there is genuine concern for his well-being, not just in a veterinary-hygiene sense, but as a moral, integrated personality.

The problem of integration, like most human problems, has a venerable past. The modern version goes back at least 160 years and was precipitated by an historical paradox: the twin births of modern individualism and modern industrialism. The former brought about a deep concern for and a passionate interest in the individual and his personal rights. The latter brought about increased mechanization of organized activity. Competition between the two has intensified as each decade promises more freedom and hope for man and more stunning achievements for technology. I believe that our society *has* opted for more humanistic and democratic values, however unfulfilled they may be in practice. It will "buy" these values even at loss in efficiency because it feels it can now afford the loss.

2 *Social influence.* This problem is essentially one of power and how power is distributed. It is a complex issue and alive with controversy, partly because of an ethical component and partly because studies of leadership and power distribution can be interpreted in many ways, and almost always in ways which coincide with one's biases (including a cultural leaning toward democracy).

The problem of power has to be seriously reconsidered because of dramatic situational changes which make the possibility of one-man rule not necessarily "bad" but impractical. I refer to changes in top management's role.

Peter Drucker, over twelve years ago, listed 41 major responsibilities of the chief executive and declared that "90 percent of the trouble we are having with the chief executive's job is rooted in our superstition of the one-man chief." Many factors make one-man control obsolete, among them: the broadening product base of industry; impact of new technology; the scope of international operation; the separation of management from ownership; the rise of trade unions and general education. The real power of the "chief" has been eroding in most organizations even though both he and the organization cling to the older concept.

3 *Collaboration.* This is the problem of managing and resolving conflicts. Bureaucratically, it grows out of the very same social process of conflict and stereotyping that has divided nations and communities. As organizations become more complex, they fragment and divide, building tribal patterns and symbolic codes which often work to exclude others (secrets and jargon, for example) and on occasion to exploit differences for inward (and always fragile) harmony.

Recent research is shedding new light on the problem of conflict. Psychologist Robert R. Blake in his stunning experiments has shown how simple it is to induce conflict, how difficult to arrest it. Take two groups of people who have never before been together, and give them a task which will be judged by an impartial jury. In less than an hour, each group devolves into a tightly-knit band with all the symptoms of an "in group." They regard their product as a "masterwork" and the other group's as "commonplace" at best. "Other" becomes "enemy." "We are good, they are bad; we are right, they are wrong."

Jaap Rabbie, conducting experiments on intergroup conflict at the University of Utrecht, has been amazed by the ease with which conflict and stereotype develop. He brings into an experimental room two groups and distributes green name tags and pens to one group, red pens and tags to the other. The two groups do not compete; they do not even interact. They are only in sight of each other while they silently complete a questionnaire. Only 10 minutes are needed to activate defensiveness and fear, reflected in the hostile and irrational perceptions of both "reds" and "greens."

4 *Adaptation.* This problem is caused by

our turbulent environment. The pyramid structure of bureaucracy, where power is concentrated at the top, seems the perfect way to "run a railroad." And for the routine tasks of the 19th and early 20th centuries, bureaucracy was (in some respects it still is) a suitable social arrangement. However, rather than a placid and predictable environment, what predominates today is a dynamic and uncertain one where, there is a deepening interdependence among economic, scientific, educational, social and political factors in the society.

5 *Revitalization.* This is the problem of growth and decay. As Alfred North Whitehead has said: "The art of free society consists first in the maintenance of the symbolic code, and secondly, in the fearlessness of revision. . . . Those societies which cannot combine reverence to their symbols with freedom of revision must ultimately decay. . . ."

Growth and decay emerge as the penultimate conditions of contemporary society. Organizations, as well as societies, must be concerned with those social structures that engender buoyancy, resilience and a "fearlessness of revision."

I introduce the term "revitalization" to embrace all the social mechanisms that stagnate and regenerate, as well as the process of this cycle. The elements of revitalization are:

1 An ability to learn from experience and to codify, store and retrieve the relevant knowledge.

2 An ability to "learn how to learn," that is, to develop methods for improving the learning process.

3 An ability to acquire and use feedback mechanisms on performance, in short, to be self-analytical.

4 An ability to direct one's own destiny.

These qualities have a good deal in common with what John Gardner calls "self-renewal." For the organization, it means conscious attention to its own evolution. Without a planned methodology and explicit direction, the enterprise will not realize its potential.

Integration, distribution of power, collaboration, adaptation and *revitalization*—these are the major human problems of the next 25 years. How organizations cope with and manage these tasks will undoubtedly determine the viability of the enterprise.

Against this background I should like to set forth some of the conditions that will dictate organizational life in the next two or three decades.

1 *The environment.* Rapid technological change and diversification will lead to more and more partnerships between government and business. It will be a truly mixed economy. Because of the immensity and expense of the projects, there will be fewer identical units competing in the same markets and organizations will become more interdependent.

The four main features of this environment are:

Interdependence rather than competition.
Turbulence and uncertainty rather than readiness and certainty.
Large-scale rather than small-scale enterprises.
Complex and multinational rather than simple national enterprises.

2 *Population characteristics.* The most distinctive characteristic of our society is education. It will become even more so. Within 15 years, two thirds of our population living in metropolitan areas will have attended college. Adult education is growing even faster, probably because of the rate of professional obsolescence. The Killian report showed that the average engineer required further education only 10 years after getting his degree. It will be almost routine for the experienced physician, engineer and executive to go back to school for advanced training every two or three years. All of this education is not just "nice." It is necessary.

. One other characteristic of the population which will aid our understanding of organizations of the future is increasing job mobility. The ease of transportation, coupled with the needs of a dynamic environment, change drastically the idea of "owning" a job—or "having roots." Already 20 percent of our population change their mailing address at least once a year.

3 *Work values.* The increased level of education and mobility will change the values we place on work. People will be more intellectually committed to their jobs and will probably require more involvement, participation and autonomy.

Also, people will be more "other-oriented," taking cues for their norms and values from their immediate environment rather than tradition.

4 *Tasks and goals.* The tasks of the organi-

zation will be more technical, complicated and unprogrammed. They will rely on intellect instead of muscle. And they will be too complicated for one person to comprehend, to say nothing of control. Essentially, they will call for the collaboration of specialists in a project or a team-form of organization.

There will be a complication of goals. Business will increasingly concern itself with its adaptive or innovative-creative capacity. In addition, supragoals will have to be articulated, goals which shape and provide the foundation for the goal structure. For example, one might be a system for detecting new and changing goals; another could be a system for deciding priorities among goals.

Finally, there will be more conflict and contradiction among diverse standards for organizational effectiveness. This is because professionals tend to identify more with the goals of their profession than with those of their immediate employer. University professors can be used as a case in point. Their inside work may be a conflict between teaching and research, while more of their income is derived from outside sources, such as foundations and consultant work. They tend not to be good "company men" because they divide their loyalty between their professional values and organizational goals.

5 *Organization.* The social structure of organizations of the future will have some unique characteristics. The key word will be "temporary." There will be adaptive, rapidly changing *temporary* systems. These will be task forces organized around problems-to-be-solved by groups of relative strangers with diverse professional skills. The group will be arranged on an organic rather than mechanical model; they will evolve in response to a problem rather than to programmed role expectations. The executive thus becomes a coordinator or "linking pin" between various task forces. He must be a man who can speak the polyglot jargon of research, with skills to relay information and to mediate between groups. People will be evaluated not vertically according to rank and status, but flexibly and functionally according to skill and professional training. Organizational charts will consist of project groups rather than stratified functional groups. (This trend is already visible in the aerospace and construction industries, as well as many professional and consulting firms.)

Adaptive, problem-solving, temporary systems of diverse specialists, linked together by coordinating and task-evaluating executive specialists in an organic flux—this is the organization form that will gradually replace bureaucracy as we know it. As no catchy phrase comes to mind, I call this an organic-adaptive structure. Organizational arrangements of this sort may not only reduce the intergroup conflicts mentioned earlier; it may also induce honest-to-goodness creative collaboration.

6 *Motivation.* The organic-adaptive structure should increase motivation and thereby effectiveness, because it enhances satisfactions intrinsic to the task. There is a harmony between the educated individual's need for tasks that are meaningful, satisfactory and creative and a flexible organizational structure.

There will also be, however, reduced commitment to work groups, for these groups will be, as I have already mentioned, transient structures. I would predict that in the organic-adaptive system, people will learn to develop quick and intense relationships on the job, and learn to bear the loss of more enduring work relationships. Because of the added ambiguity of roles, time will have to be spent on continual rediscovery of the appropriate organizational mix.

I think that the future I describe is not necessarily a "happy" one. Coping with rapid change, living in temporary work systems, developing meaningful relations and then breaking them—all augur social strains and psychological tensions. Teaching how to live with ambiguity, to identify with the adaptive process, to make a virtue out of contingency, and to be self-directing—these will be the tasks of education, the goals of maturity, and the achievement of the successful individual.

In these new organizations of the future, participants will be called upon to use their minds more than at any other time in history. Fantasy, imagination and creativity will be legitimate in ways that today seem strange. Social structures will no longer be instruments of psychic repression but will increasingly promote play and freedom on behalf of curiosity and thought.

One final word: While I forecast the structure and value coordinates for organizations of the future and contend that they are inevitable, this should not bar any of us from giving the inevitable a little push. The French moralist may be right in saying that there are no delightful marriages, just good ones; it is possible that if managers and scientists continue to get their heads together in organizational revitalization, they *might* develop delightful organizations—just possibly.

I started with a quote from de Tocqueville and I think it would be fitting to end with one: "I am tempted to believe that what we call necessary institutions are often no more than institutions to which we have grown accustomed. In matters of social constitution, the field of possibilities is much more extensive than men living in their various societies are ready to imagine."

READING 2

THE DECLINE OF THE HIERARCHY IN INDUSTRIAL ORGANIZATIONS *

William H. Read

Has today's executive really faced the impact of technological changes on corporate structure and function? Although such changes force industrial leaders to rethink and readjust relationships between manager and manager, manager and specialist, and specialist and specialist, deeply-rooted organizational tradition may make the transition a stressful one.

THE BUREAUCRATIC TRADITION

The bureaucratic tradition, and the set of beliefs that underlie it, emerged from nineteenth century notions about the theory and practice of administration, and has survived since then despite progressive changes in the administrative process. It deals with the nature of authority relations, leader and follower interaction, the division of administration into "higher," "middle," and "lower" management, and the way in which business organizations function.

* *Reprinted by permission from* Business Horizons, *Fall, 1965.*

Four interrelated assumptions are contained in the bureaucratic tradition. *First,* the central, crucial, and important business of an organization is conducted up and down the vertical hierarchy. This general process can be described as information organized into certain patterns and passed upward through management levels, while decisions and directives based on this information are passed downward. In this way, according to tradition, organizations function. *Second,* the bureaucratic tradition sees the corporate body as something like the human body in that it has a kind of central nervous system (chain of command) with a spine going up the back, and a brain on top (top management), which does most, if not all, of the directing and steering of important matters. *Third,* the vertical (authority) levels of an organization roughly correspond to levels or gradations of talent and competence. In general, the higher up one goes, the more talent, the more daring, and the more dedication one finds in that organization's mission. *Fourth,* by far the most important single type of relationship in an organization is the superior-subordinate one. If this relationship is healthy and productive, success follows naturally, according to the bureaucratic tradition, since it is in the vertical dimension of organizations that the business is done.

It should be emphasized that however facetiously they have been stated here, these assumptions have provided the philosophical fabric that has united many diverse activities and individuals into what we have come to know as the corporation—people, performing functions, directed toward the achievement of specified goals.

What then is wrong with the bureaucratic tradition? Surely the authority or "line" or administrative system is an absolutely necessary component of a business organization. But is it sufficient? Or rather, is it as sufficient now as it once was? According to some modern scholars of administration,[1] the authority system, the "vertical" of a modern business organization, tends to remain the dominant, at times almost exclusive, structural feature of the modern corporation, long after technological change has created an urgent need for equally powerful organizational machinery to smooth out the lateral flow of decisions, requests, and data.

Perhaps this protest is a bit too strong. But the contemporary business executive should now be willing to entertain the idea that the current system or pattern of managerial action in the modern corporation is rapidly becoming outmoded and considerably overemphasized. Irresistible pressures are now being exerted on corporations, even moderate-sized ones, to change. The pressure stems chiefly from technological change—from the fast-paced revolution in the type and use of hardware, in the type, use, and processing of information, in the systematization and integration of even the simplest jobs and processes and, particularly, in the computerization of an enormous range of business decisions.

These changes are forcing a new appraisal of the relations, authority and otherwise, between people in a modern corporation. Yet many management people are resisting this force—either actively or passively, consciously or unconsciously. Traditions resist change and

[1] F. J. Jasinski, "Adapting Organization to New Technology," Harvard Business Review, XXXVII, no. 1 (January-February, 1959), 79–86.

so do people; old ways of doing things, established ways of thinking and reacting, are always more comfortable.

A NEW TRADITION

Perhaps then we ought to look again at the bureaucratic tradition, and counter its four major sets of assumptions with a new set. *First,* the central, crucial, and important business of organizations is increasingly shifting from up and down to "sideways"—from the vertical or line organization to the *lateral* or *horizontal. Second,* vertical levels of an organization no longer represent roughly the distribution or gradation of talent or brains in an organization. More and more, talent is where you find it, and both talent and creativity are quite often boxed off to one side with only fuzzy provisions for them to function in the mainstream of the organization. The reference here is to highly skilled and talented specialists who have inherited the title "staff group." *Third,* superior-subordinate relationships in an organization, though obviously important, no longer guarantee by their harmony that everything will be all right any more than there is a guarantee that the human body will function effectively with a healthy nervous system but with injured organs.

In a nutshell, the structure of corporations is changing and in fact must change to cope with the impact of complex and sophisticated technological systems. Complex information flow systems, plus the staggering rate of transformation of hand-operated or semi-automatic production and office machinery into automatic, centrally-controlled machine systems, are creating a proliferation of highly skilled specialists, and an even greater proliferation of need for their services. Not only the size, but the skill and influence of these specialized staff groups are deepening and accelerating. The significant point is that these specialists do not fit neatly into a chain-of-command system, cannot easily be lumped together and called "staff," cannot wait for their expert advice to be approved at a higher level, and cannot function effectively if their expertise is shrugged off by recalcitrant old-timers. The corporation manager needs them and needs them badly, just as the expert badly needs the "generalists" among management who can grasp, evaluate, and coordinate specialist work.

These changes now taking place make the

effective coordination of specialists the major problem of effective organizational functioning. They are increasingly forcing the manager in the modern corporation to look, work, and think sideways—to establish working relationships laterally with his specialist peers and to de-emphasize vertical relationships with his boss or subordinate.

Some Evidence of Change

For some time now it has been evident that lateral or horizontal relations are more vital to the efficiency of a production organization than was formerly recognized—and that the peer-colleague is the key person in the organizational world of the executive. Yet in our concern for superior-subordinate relations, our heavy emphasis on "man management," and the willingness of industrial leaders to spend enormous sums on human relations training, we have neglected this dimension of organizations.

Some years ago, a group of social scientists conducted an exhaustive study of jobs and worker-supervisor relations in a U.S. automotive plant.[2] They discovered that, contrary to expectations, the boss (foreman) actually did not exert much influence in the workplace. His role was important, but much more as a technician than as a supervisor, much more as a troubleshooter and human monitor of a complex flow system than as a leader. More important than this, though, his major function seemed to be to get the operators fast help when they needed it: help from specialists on or close to his own administrative level—methods men, maintenance experts, and production schedulers. The study indicated that the system itself did a good part of the supervising; the foreman, who had little direct personal contact with the operators, served as liaison between them and the system, and between them and the experts.

A somewhat similar result was seen in a more recent study of manager-worker relations in a textile mill.[3] As mechanization in the mill increased, a corresponding increase occurred in the rate of cross-communication between supervisors on the one hand and other supervisors and experts on the other. The most important function of the supervisor was not to link management and the worker, not even to coordinate closely with management levels, but to short-circuit and bypass upper-level management in order to get fast, on-the-spot decisions from specialists. The absence of managerial intervention, not the effectiveness of it, was the key to success.

In view of the deeply rooted traditions of administration outlined above, these events represent a staggering change in thinking, action, and decision making in organizations. It means that the classical management function of motivating subordinates, making decisions on the basis of collated data passed upward, and introducing changes in procedure may well be in the process of atrophy. As one writer has recently stated, we are headed for a "working society of technical co-equals" and the "line of demarcation between the leader and the led has (already) become fuzzy."[4]

The Obsolete Square

In this vein, consider a very simple example of old, transitional, and new ways in which decisions, requests for services, and other messages are routed in a production or office department. In the production department of a certain manufacturing organization, a large-scale changeover had been made from semiautomatic to automatic machinery. For maintenance service in all but the simplest problems, prior to the change, the established procedure had been for the operator to route the request upward through his own foreman, who signalled the maintenance chief, who designated the appropriate serviceman (Figure 2-1). This practice was continued after the introduction of high-speed machinery, in order to maintain control, and expensive delays resulted. The routing system, diagramed below, had become obsolete and dysfunctional.

The system was soon streamlined by introducing a diagonal route (Figure 2-2), which eliminated one delay point (the operator's boss) and, incidentally, almost completely bypassed the traditional chain of command.

[2] C. R. Walker, R. H. Guest, and A. N. Turner, The Foreman on the Assembly Line *(Cambridge: Harvard University Press, 1956).*

[3] R. L. Simpson, *"Vertical and Horizontal Communication in Formal Organizations,"* Administrative Science Quarterly, IV *(1959), 188–96.*

[4] J. A. Raffaele, *"Automation and the Coming Diffusion of Power in Industry,"* Personnel, XXXIX *(1962), 30.*

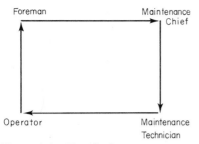

Figure 2-1   The obsolete square.

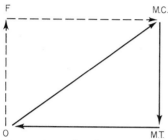

Figure 2-2   The diagonal.

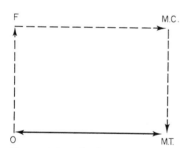

Figure 2-3   The horizontal line.

At present, management is somewhat nervously considering a complete short-circuiting of the command chain in order to eliminate delays and speed the entire process. The horizontal, direct route will have replaced the authority structure in one small segment of the organization.

Figure 2-3 illustrates, however roughly, the crucial importance not only of lowering the coordination function in the organization, but also of developing a formally sanctioned, non-authority, or semi-authority, relationship between production operator and specialist. The operator must now be more than an operator; he must be an accomplished coordinator.

Horizontal and diagonal coordination, always important, will now be the major human

problem of the new industrial revolution. Yet, unlike the problem of supervision, no clear program, no ideology, and no techniques have been developed for handling it. In many ways, it is a greater problem than that of authority relations, which has occupied management for a century or so. Relations between expert and manager, between expert and expert, and between manager and manager are in some ways more vulnerable than those between boss and subordinate. A major hurdle is presented by the dichotomy between men of thought and men of action (expert and manager), a natural division that rarely exists between a man and his supervisor. Because of radical differences in their training and background, it is very difficult for a production chief to grasp the function and outlook of a system analyst, and vice versa. The problem is even greater with the expert-to-expert relationship, that is, it is even harder for the personnel psychologist to see eye to eye with experts involved in the computerization of an office. Yet both must cope with the problem of radical changes in manpower and skills in a particular office setting.

ALTERNATIVES FOR CHANGE

What broad courses of planning and action are open to industrial leaders in dealing with the impact of technology? The first alternative is to change people: their attitudes, perspectives, and outlooks. The revolution now taking place in our industrial system in both factory and office is going to require a different pattern of management skills. In addition, these changes are going to demand a different type of specialist, with a broader perspective, with as sharp an insight into human and organizational relationships as into mathematical and mechanical ones, and even more crucial, with the vision and wisdom to deal with the greater influence that will be his. Retraining and reeducation, then, suggest one major course for preparatory action. The company training classroom and the university campus can be equally effective settings for manager and specialist to interact and to exchange skills and outlooks, with the university offering special short-term training programs.

A second line of preparatory action is to change the form of the organization. The reorganization of tasks, the restructuring of formal organizational relationships, and even the phasing out of some aspects of the traditional hierarchical form of organization have already been accomplished in a few of the more technologically advanced U.S. corporations. In Task Force and Weapons System[5] management, for example, rigid spans of control, and sharp hierarchical leveling, are being abandoned or severely modified in favor of closely coordinated, integrated teams or project groups that cut across functional levels, largely circumvent chains of command, and contain often astounding degrees of skill-mix. The result is a sink or swim confrontation of the problems of horizontal coordination. In an even newer organization form, Rotated Organization Struc-

ture (ROS),[6] management functions are completely bifurcated into planning and operating, with rotation, by time period or project, of personnel between these two functions. Thus specialists are *ipso facto* responsible for doing as well as planning. Management generalists, conversely, must plan as well as do.

It is, in short, quite possible that the only truly effective methods for preventing, or coping with, problems of coordination and communication in our changing technology will be found in new arrangements of people and tasks, in arrangements which sharply break with the bureaucratic tradition. In either case, by changing people or changing organizations, a reappraisal of our traditional methods of achieving organizational goals is urgently in order.

[5] *Fremont E. Kast and James Rosenzweig, "Weapons System Management and Organizational Relationships,"* Journal of the Academy of Management, *IV (1961), 188–205.*

[6] *Ronald J. Ross, "Rotating Planners and Doers,"* Harvard Business Review, *XL (1962), 105–16.*

READING 3

MATRIX ORGANIZATION *

John F. Mee

A matrix organizational design has evolved in the flow of aerospace technology; changing conditions have caused managers to create new relationships of established organizational concepts and principles. A matrix organization is used to establish a flexible and adaptable system of resources and procedures to achieve a series of project objectives. The figure on the next page is a conceptual framework for a matrix type of organization. It illustrates the coordinated or matrix system of relationships among the functions essential to market, finance, and produce highly specialized goods or services.

From a divisionalized organization structure has emerged a new way of thinking and working to create products dependent upon advanced research and urgency for completion. Time and technology factors forced a more efficient utilization of human talents and facilitating resources.

* *Reprinted by permission from* Business Horizons, *Summer, 1964.*

The traditional divisional type of organization permits a flow of work to progress among autonomous functional units of a specific division. A division manager is responsible for total programs of work involving the products of his division. In a matrix organization, the divisional manager has the same responsibility, authority, and accountability for results. Differences occur in the division of work performed as well as in the allocation of authority, responsibility, and accountability for the completion of work projects.

If work performed by an operating division of a company is applied to standardized products or services with high volume, there is no need to consider a matrix organizational design. The total work can flow through the division with each functional group adding its value and facilitation to the completion of the production process. The total work can flow along and among the functional groups of production to a market. The emphasis is on the efficiency of the flow of work.

It is when work performed is for specific

project contracts that a matrix organization can be used effectively. If the market for a product is a single customer such as the U.S. Air Force or an industrial firm with a prime governmental contract, the production emphasis changes to the completion of action for a specific work project instead of a flow of work on production programs for product volume. In the illustration of the aerospace division (Figure 3-1), the emphasis is on the completion of specific work projects, namely, Venus project, Mars project, and Saturn project. Additional projects may be added as new contracts are signed by the marketing group. As projects are completed or

abolished, they are deleted from the organization; it is a fluid organization.

A matrix type of organization is built around specific projects. A manager is given the authority, responsibility, and accountability for the completion of the project in accordance with the time, cost, quality, and quantity provisions in the project contract. The line organization develops from the project and leaves the previous line functions in a support relationship to the project line organization.

The project manager is assigned the number of personnel with the essential qualifications from the functional departments for the dura-

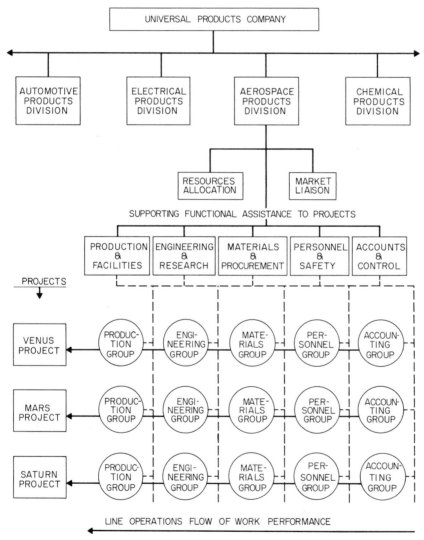

Figure 3-1   Matrix organization. (Aerospace Division).

tion of the project. Thus the project organization is composed of the manager and functional personnel groups. With responsibility and accountability for the successful completion of the contract, the project manager has the authority for work design, assignment of functional group personnel, and the determination of procedural relationships. He has the authority to reward personnel with promotions, salary increases, and other incentives while the project is in progress. He also has the authority to relieve personnel from the functional group assignments. Upon completion of the project, the functional group personnel return to the functional departments for reassignment, or transfer to other divisions or training programs to develop their skills and knowledge. The project manager is also available for reassignment by the division manager or company president.

Management by project objectives or results is paramount to the way of thinking and working in a matrix type of organization. The group organizational personnel perform the line operational work to complete the project. The department functional personnel give support assistance to the line projects such as policy guidance, technical advice, and administrative services. In a matrix organizational chart, the line operations may be illustrated horizontally as the functional groups are aligned to achieve a specific project. The support assistance from the functional departments appears vertically in relationship to the series of projects undertaken by the division.

The concept of a matrix organization entails an organizational system designed as a "web of relationships" rather than a line and staff relationship of work performance. The web of relationships is aimed at starting and completing specific projects. An over-all divisional function of resource allocation for multiple projects determines the priority of resources for specific projects and measures progress against contract requirements.

American managers possess a proud record of ingenuity in creating new organizational schemes to adapt to changing technological and economic requirements. The matrix organizational design is no exception. It permits a higher degree of specialization for human talents with maximum efficiency of operations. New techniques for systems management, information economics, and information systems, as well as improved production planning and control systems, are developing to advance more sophisticated organizational relationships of work, people, and coordinated procedures. Managerial and technical personnel will require new knowledge and skills as well as modified attitudes.

Unless managers and operating personnel are educated and trained to work in the developing organizational designs, they can suffer frustrations, emotional disturbances, and loss of motivation. Working in an environment characterized by change as projects are started and completed is not as comfortable and secure as performing a continuing function in a more stable standardized work flow situation.

Although the matrix organization emerged to improve work performance in the aerospace industry, other alert industrial managers can adapt the concept for uses in new product or market developments in a marketing dominated economy.

READING 4

PRODUCT MANAGEMENT: PANACEA OR PANDORA'S BOX*

Robert M. Fulmer

Despite its climb to popularity during the recent "marketing revolution," product management has failed to satisfy the hopes of some of its more optimistic adopters. The divergence between the highly touted theoretical potentials of product management and the conflict and confusion which occasionally followed its adoption has led some observers and practitioners to conclude that this organizational innovation is an impractical, unworkable, and unrealistic method of centering responsibility for the success of a product or product line. Yet, without question, there are several large, multiproduct companies where product management has provided a remarkably efficient method for coordinating and focusing the functional activities of the firm so as to gain a maximum amount of attention and activity for each product marketed.

How can the same concept be both a panacea and a Pandora's box? A cursory analysis

* Reprinted from California Management Review, vol. VII, no. 4, Summer, 1965. Copyright 1965 by The Regents of The University of California.

of published reports and empirical observations of product management in practice reveal that most of the difficulties mentioned revolve around the following problems: authority, selection, and definition.

Authority: how much and what kind? While it is impossible to give a universal answer to this question, it is unlikely that companies which exact responsibility for total product success without granting commensurate authority can expect the same results as a firm where the product manager is used as a coordinative center of authority to insure unified effort on behalf of each product. Similarly, it is doubtful that a staff assistant, salesman, or clerk can be as effective in working for a product's over-all success as the "president of a company within a company." Yet, positions with such varying degrees of authority are often discussed together under the heading of product management. This article will not attempt to provide an exact recipe for the authority and responsibility to be given product managers, but an overview of the existing spectrum of product-oriented positions will be given and conclusions drawn as to the practicality of this indiscriminate classification.

Selection: traits or training? Obviously, the ability to delegate authority and exact responsibility will depend on the talents of the employees involved and the degree to which these talents have been cultivated or utilized. There is no magic in the product management concept; consequently, the idea can be no more effective than the men who fill the positions.

Some companies find it desirable to recruit men expressly for development as product managers. Other firms feel that prior experience in one of the company's functional departments is essential. Certain general managerial traits such as the ability to accept responsibility, to think creatively and practically, to act quickly, and to work harmoniously with other departments are necessary. In every instance, a period of training directed toward the requirements of product management will increase effectiveness. Staffing problems are as unique as individual companies; therefore, any detailed analysis would be applicable only in the situation studied. The reservoir of available managerial talent certainly must be considered in any attempt to plan or evaluate the use of product management.

Definition: does everyone understand? Almost every problem found in product management literature relates, in some way, to improper or misunderstood definitions. A primary step in the solution of difficulties connected with authority delegation and selection is a definite statement of the requirements of the position. With this as a foundation, authority can be delegated and individuals can be selected and trained in view of the requirements. While a general understanding of the terms used in discussing product management is important for all persons interested in this aspect of organization, the need for specificity is paramount for intrafirm understanding. In other words, if a term is misused, it can still prove of value if all personnel within a firm have the same understanding of its meaning.

I will attempt to move toward possible clarifications of these problems by analyzing the various ways in which different practitioners and scholars approach them, discarding the obviously incorrect, and discussing the relative merits of the acceptable theories.

A CONFUSING HISTORY

Origin of product management. The history of product management provides an interesting insight into its initiating philosophy and can serve as a yardstick by which the later developments may be compared. Product management in its initial form appears to have first been practiced as brand management at Procter and Gamble nearly forty years ago. Since that time, product management has produced an outstanding genealogy (probably including such ramifications as project management, task teams, and, of course, brand management in its various forms). Some of these successors bear little resemblance to the original form of this organizational innovation. Perhaps the multiplicity of members in the product management family has made it difficult to pinpoint the exact birth of the idea. Certainly no aspect of this subject provides a better illustration of the misunderstanding and confusion which pervade the literature. Consider, for example, several absolute statements as to the origin of this idea.

The concept of product management is not new. Probably it originated in the retail trade, in this case in the department stores.[1]

Since the product manager concept was originally developed by General Electric in the early 1950's, most large companies have adopted the approach in one way or another.[2]

The product manager originated accidentally— first as an assistant sales manager with an interest in a particular product or group of products.[3]

An analysis of the concept's history will provide some clues. The product manager's job was created primarily to fill a critical need. In large, multiproduct companies, it has always been difficult to be certain that each product received the attention and support it merited from each of various functional activities of the business, especially manufacturing, marketing, and sales. . . . Therefore, to meet this need, the product manager form of organization was created.[4]

It has been suggested that the rapid expansion of product lines and the need for developing specialized marketing strategies about specific products were the key points indicating a need for the product management function. ... Initially the task of the product manager was one of a coordinator, trying to harmonize the manufacturing and marketing activities associated with his products. Gradually authority was delegated to him to make decisions regarding product improvement, packaging, pricing, field selling, advertising, etc. As authority was increased, the final responsibility for profits and market position was delegated to him.[5]

Often mistakenly thought of as a comparatively new marketing creature, in Procter and Gamble, the brand manager goes back to 1931, when now-chairman Neil McElroy formalized that role in the company.[6]

It is possible that the idea of having one individual with primary responsibility for a group of products originated in the department store; however, the department head of a retail store is no more a product manager than is the production chief of a factory producing similar items or any manager with responsibility for some phase of the life cycle of one or more related products.

General Electric is often credited with ushering in the marketing concept with its reorganization in the early 1950's. While this distinction is somewhat dubious, without question there were companies employing product managers before the 1950's.

The position referred to as "product manager" in some companies may have evolved from "an assistant sales manager with an interest in a particular product or group of products." There is, however, little evidence that this title was so applied before 1928, and, as will be discussed later, there is reason to challenge the accuracy of using the title to describe specialized sales positions.

CREATION OF THE BRAND MAN

Although, and perhaps because, they lack any degree of specificity as to date and source of origin, it is difficult to question the statements cited from Ames or Schiff and Mellman previously quoted. There should be universal agreement that the job of product manager was created to fill the need to provide vigorous product-by-product leadership for multiproduct companies. This view is supported in the *Printers' Ink* article of September 28, 1962, in which Procter and Gamble's Neil McElroy is credited with originating that company's brand-

man organization in 1931. Actually the brand-man system began its evolution in this company even earlier. In January, 1928, Mr. C. C. Uhling was made Procter and Gamble's first brand manager when Lava soap was assigned to him. Later, brand-man assignments were made for Oxydol and Camay.[7] In 1931, the recommendation of McElroy was instrumental in refining the brand-man system and in making it a company-wide concept. This refinement consisted basically in the creation of the brand group hierarchy composed of an assistant brand man, who was to perform much of the detail involved in the management of a particular brand and to serve as an understudy of his superior; the brand man; and the brand-group supervisors, each responsible for reviewing the work of two to four brand managers, who reported to the head of the brand-promotion division.[8] To date, this company has enjoyed almost unparalleled success with little change in orientation or scope of the concept.

It is impossible to determine all the factors which influenced the thinking of those associated with the birth and development of this idea. However, it is possible that the reorganization of Du Pont and General Motors several years before had helped initiate the thought processes which led to this evolution by providing a working example of the product-oriented divisionalization. Ease of coordinating, by brand, the activities of advertising agencies was another possible contributing factor.[9] Certainly, the primary motivation appears to have been the desire to guarantee individual management for each of a number of products.

WHAT DOES THE TITLE MEAN?

What is a product manager?   Perhaps a portion of the problems besetting product management stem from a fundamental lack of understanding or confusion about what is meant by the term. There is a wide spectrum of meanings attached to this term which were not implied at its birth.

One extreme of the range is found in firms such as the National Biscuit Company where one product manager handles everything that pertains to the products except the actual selling—among his responsibilities are product quality, packaging, marketing, advertising, and promotion programs. One product manager handles these responsibilities for Dromedary cake mixes, nut rolls, pimientos, dates, fruits, and peels.[10] In essence this job could be accurately referred to as vice-president of a product division or simply as a division manager; the same holds true where the term "product manager" is used to describe General Electric's general managers. This is somewhat equivalent to calling the head of General Motors' Chevrolet Division a product manager. To avoid confusion, it is wise to differentiate between the titles of the executive who is in charge of a multiproduct division and the manager who has responsibility for a single product.

Examples of companies where real product or brand managers have extensive responsibility would include the following:

> At **Pillsbury,** the man who bears the title, brand manager, has total accountability for results. He directs the marketing of his product as if it were his own business. Production does its job, and finance keeps the profit figures. Otherwise, the brand manager has total responsibility for marketing his product. This responsibility encompasses pricing, commercial research, competitive activity, home service, and publicity coordination, legal details, budgets, advertising plans, sales promotion, and execution of plans.[11]

> Each of **Kimberly-Clark's** brand managers is responsible for drawing up complete marketing programs for his brand. ... In addition (to serving as advertising manager for his product), the brand manager is responsible for recommending marketing objectives for his brand, planning marketing strategy, drawing proposed budgets, initiating new projects and programs, and coordinating the work of all functional units concerned with the production, financing, and marketing of the product.[12]

> At **Colgate-Palmolive,** product managers are responsible for developing plans and programs that will establish brand leadership and enlarge the current and long-range share of market and profits for their brands. These plans include advertising and promotional programs and budgets, selection of distribution channels, forecasts of sales and inventory requirements, forecasts of manufacturing costs, and, as final objectives, projections of profit and share of market on the brands.[13]

Men employed for this work (at **Proc-** **ter and Gamble**) are trained to accept the responsibility for the effectiveness of the over-all advertising and promotion effort on an important nationally advertised brand.... These positions involve working with many company departments, including research and development on product development, the sales department on the development of promotions and also with the advertising agency on all phases of consumer planning for the brand.[14]

At the other end of the spectrum from these consumer-oriented producers are some companies such as **Minneapolis-Honeywell** where:

> ... the divisional executives in charge of selling temperature controls to the school market decided to appoint a "product manager" ... who was charged with the broad responsibility of securing more business in this field.... Basically a salesman ... sales management must select its man with great care.[15]

In his study of the semi-conductor industry, Bucklin observed that product managers were frequently required to spend 50 percent of their time in calling on accounts.[16] Ames refers to an anonymous company where a product manager's role is really limited to maintaining sales statistics and performing a variety of high-grade clerical tasks.[17] Mauser makes the general claim that: "Sales managers for products may be given the simple title of product manager."[18]

R. H. Buskirk recognizes the divergent uses of the product manager title and asserts that: "The dimensions of his job vary widely from company to company, sometimes embracing all the activities of product management and sometimes being limited to the sales promotion of the products in his care."[19]

It appears that Professor Buskirk believes that a product manager does not necessarily handle the work of product management, for he defines product management as:

> The planning, direction, and control of all phases of the life cycle of products, including the creation or discovery of ideas for new products, the screening of such ideas, the coordination of the work of research and physical development of products, their packaging and branding,

their introduction on the market, their market development, their modification, the discovery of new uses for them, their repair and servicing, and their deletion.[20]

From a descriptive standpoint, there is no doubt that in many companies "product managers" find their positions much more narrow than the description of product management. A normative view, however, should place considerable emphasis on bringing these two concepts together. The problem of management semantics, eloquently recognized by Col. Lyndall Urwick,[21] will continue to rear its ugly head and breed confusion and misunderstanding as long as commonly used terms such as these two have such a diversity of meaning and application.

While it is impossible to generalize from one article, a recent German publication[22] indicates that such confusion may not be so prevalent in that country. While the brand manager system is practiced only by some companies which are based in the United States and a few German firms in the food, detergent, and electrical industries, it is evidently practiced quite satisfactorily. If the German experience is indeed less chaotic than product management history in the United States, it may be due to the fact that United States companies are not likely to export the concept until they have eliminated most of the major difficulties in domestic practice. Consequently, a descriptive definition of product management in Germany should provide helpful insight into a type considered hardy enough to export. A review of the article suggests the following areas of product management activity:

1 Marketing analysis (product, packaging, price, assortment, channels of distribution).
2 Setting of marketing goals.
3 Long- and short-range planning and budgeting.
4 Coordination of work done by departments within a company as well as by "outsiders" (marketing research, selling, advertising, public relations, production, technical research, financing).
5 Control.[23]

In a report prepared for the Financial Executives' Research Foundation, Schiff and Mellman describe the product manager as "the executive responsible for product manage-

ment."[24] This definition may appear to be circular reasoning, but it may be expanded to say that a product manager must manage something; if he does not exercise the managerial functions of planning, direction, and control in relation to the entire scope of a product's immediate existence, he is something less than a product manager and should be appropriately renamed. Though overly simple, this is infinitely superior to saying that a product manager does not necessarily manage a product or that he may manage only one aspect of its existence. This definition does not require that all phases of a product's life cycle (from idea origination to termination of production) be exclusively the domain of one individual, but it does require management as one of the identifying characteristics of a product manager.

The product manager and his authority.

> The (product manager) concept is an organization anomaly in that it violates a proven management precept—that responsibility should always be matched by equivalent authority ... (he is) a member of the management group with high level responsibility for getting a product to market without any line authority over the full range of activities required to get the job done.[25]

An equally extreme position concerning the product manager is taken by R. H. Jacobs who asserts:

> His is not, in essence, a management job but a staff job whose sole responsibility is to secure wider sales of one or more specific items in the line.[26]

Practically speaking, the major problem in applying the product-manager concept may well be how much and what kind of authority to delegate. The quotations cited above indicate that little, if any, line authority is available to the product manager to carry out his myriad responsibilities. Bucklin found that the lack of real authority was the basis for many of the problems encountered by product managers in the semi-conductor firms.[27] *Printers' Ink* reports that, at Merck & Co., "each product manager is a staff member whose primary function is to plan for the growth and profitability of his markets."[28] The same publication generalizes:

> Few companies sharply delineate the product manager's area of operations, as between line and staff function; most of them give him heavy responsibility, though not with commensurate authority.[29]

It is small wonder that the product manager concept has recently been receiving sharp criticism. It is impossible to imagine that a manager can coordinate and manage all aspects of the life cycle of a product with his hands tied in a manner such as described above. Fortunately, this situation is not universal. In those companies which give the product manager the responsibility for product management, there appears to be general agreement that such responsibility must be matched with comparable authority. At least the product manager is not always an "organization anomaly." Professor Edward Bursk has well summarized:

> We have reached the point where we need solid action that cuts across the traditional, functional lines of marketing, finance, manufacturing, research, and so on. Finance may have to consider the desirability of capitalizing initial heavy promotional expenses, manufacturing may have to build inventories faster than is apparently economical.... All in all, there must be one man or one office to see that all these steps are taken as part of a unified effort.... Those in charge may be merely in a staff capacity, or may have varying degrees of line authority depending on how far this concept (usually referred to as product or brand management) has developed.[30]

In a similar vein, Professor Hepner states that the product manager's job requires that he be endowed with authority to get things done:

> Product managers are a kind of "general manager."... The product manager, working under the general direction of a top manager or executive, decides how products shall be made, the quantities to be made, the chains of distribution for each, its packaging, pricing, advertising, and promotion. The product manager is

more than a coordinator—he is the final authority whose decisions affect the profits to be made from his products.[31]

A previous attempt was made to define **product manager** so as to include only those individuals who were responsible for **product management**. At this point, it is proper to add to that definition the requirement that he should also possess adequate authority to handle the needs of his position. This apparently obvious truism has not been universally understood. While this authority cannot be absolute, unlimited, or unchecked, it must exist in sufficient quantity to allow use of the product manager's specialized knowledge and abilities. Bursk's poignant implication that the amount of line authority delegated is an indication of the degree to which the product-management concept has developed should provide real understanding of the product manager's job. There are clearly many companies where the concept, while supposedly employed, is in a state of considerable immaturity.

The product manager in practice. As employed in several companies, the product manager may have line authority in one specialized area of operation—advertising, sales, etc., or perhaps more commonly, general marketing—and functional authority (a slice of delimited line authority which cuts across organizational lines)[32] for the coordination of the activities of other departments **as they relate to his product:** For example, he might be directly in charge of advertising plans for the product and at the same time work closely with liaison members of the sales, market research, legal, art, production, merchandising, and sales promotion, packaging, and public relations departments. In his dealings with these departments, he is able to direct them to supply the services necessary to insure the maximum efficiency of the marketing program for his product. Under most circumstances, the representative of the service department works with several brand or product managers and, with proper planning, should be able to handle their various demands without undue conflict.

AN EXAMPLE

To illustrate, consider a typical situation where a sales force handles all of a division's six products. The very real problem of having all six product managers requesting special emphasis for their products' fall promotion could be handled by coordinative planning or appeal to a final authority. Promotional plans for the year should spell out which brands are free to promote in each selling period. At the time of plan formulation, questions and potential conflicts should be worked out between the individual product managers working in concert with their immediate superior and the division's sales manager. While the product manager focuses the coordination of the company's functional and service activities toward his product, in this case, the marketing division manager would probably hold the final power of decision to insure over-all coordination. Should situations arise during the year which forced deviations from the plan, the division manager would again serve as the ultimate appeal. Similar situations could, of course, be presented that would apply to relations with other functional or service departments.

From the foregoing discussion, it can be seen that, since he cannot hold total line authority such as is exercised by the president of a one-product company or by the division manager of a single-product division, the optimum use of the product manager should come when he is used as coordinating executive in charge of managing all component parts of the marketing mix of one particular product or brand and subject primarily to the final coordination of a superior in charge of the entire division or company.

LIMITS OF AUTHORITY

Functional authority is never absolute; therefore, the product manager does not have complete authority over all departments in the marketing program. In dealing with production, for example, his authority would have to be limited to the range of alternatives considered by production to be technically feasible. The legal department would, of necessity, determine limits to the potential activities of the brand; market research should be free to determine what research projects are practical and likely to provide the desired information; accounting would need the ability to limit activities to the financially feasible, etc. In other words, these departments could and should set parameters of operation within which the

product manager should be free to work and, in turn, to request the services of and/or direct the activities of these departments within the limits which they themselves have set.

The authority level principle[33] (which implies that for any problem there is a level of authority at which a decision can be made for its resolution) provides one remedy for conflicts which might result from this reciprocal interdependence. Many problems can, however, be avoided by careful planning and definition of the product manager's tasks, authorities, and responsibilities.

The product manager—how far from ideal? Paradoxically, the perfect product manager is not a product manager at all. Probably the only person who would completely satisfy the definition given would be the president of a single-product firm. Obviously, the concept has wider applicability than this. Many firms have attempted to approach the ideal by adopting what is frequently referred to as the "little general manager approach." In these cases, however, there must be a "big general manager" to coordinate activities and to resolve conflicts arising from the divergent points of view held by various product managers. Other companies approach the problem by giving product managers authority only to advise. We have indicated in the preceding discussion, however, that staff specialists should not be considered in the same category as the true product manager.

As mentioned above, no product manager can possess final line authority if several executives are employed in this capacity. Similarly, if only staff authority is employed, the product manager is no longer able to manage his product. The answer obviously lies in the judicious delegation of functional authority.

While the specific responsibilities of the product manager will vary according to the needs of a particular situation or the interest of the individual company adopting the concept, the rule of thumb for allocating authority must be that the product manager should always have sufficient authority to discharge the responsibilities associated with or assigned to his position. Unless this basic tenet of management theory is recognized, the product manager can be nothing more than an "organization anomaly" completely incapable of satisfying the demands made of him. This places a large measure of the success of product management in the realm of position description; for without adequate definition at this level, commensurate authority cannot be made available.

A very similar organizational concept, although it usually has an engineering or production orientation rather than a marketing emphasis and is usually less permanent than product management, is project management. Basically,

> Project management is a general management activity encompassing planning, control, supervision, and the engineering or manufacturing involved in producing the end item. . . . The project manager has very specific objectives which, when achieved, mean the end of his function. He usually has no line authority over the organizations producing the items which he must deliver. . . . Communications must be very clear, prompt, comprehensive, and frequently cut across intercompany and intracompany lines.[34]

Baumgartner suggests that although project management had its origin during World War II, it was 1958 before companies began to set up organization structures which superimposed a horizontal project organization on vertical functional lines.[35]

Figure 4-1 shows such an organization cutting across functional lines in order to accomplish project objectives.

A more familiar method of showing the relationship of product and project managers to other departments is the so-called "grid management" approach shown in the simplest form in Figure 4-2.

In project management, as with product management, it is impossible for complete authority to be granted in the various areas of responsibility. But at the same time, absolute responsibility cannot be exacted in these areas.

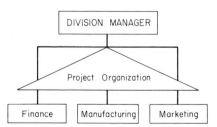

Figure 4-1 *Organizational structure.*

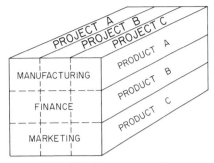

Figure 4-2 *"Grid management" structure.*

It would be incorrect to refer to a product manager as "ideal" only when he possesses complete line authority for each of his myriad responsibilities; in fact this would be chaotic even if it were possible. A situation is ideal when it functions efficiently in its particular environment.

MEANING VS. APPLICATION

Managers of products, markets, and marketing. Understanding of product management has been substantially clouded by an overlapping of several related terms. Articles referring to the concept have lumped together positions from sales promotion assistants to corporate vice-presidents under the general heading, product management. A primary emphasis of this paper has been to focus attention upon the disparity between the meaning of product management and the misapplication of this term throughout management literature. It is not enough, however, to say that the term has been incorrectly used, or to say that a spade should be called a spade. Some suggestion should be made as to the proper classification of those positions which have been shorn of the "product manager" appellation. Without attempting to use a currently popular buzzword to cover a multitude of positions and without particular emphasis on originality, why not merely call these positions what they are? For example, where one authority states, "Sales managers for products may be given the simple title of product manager,"[36] would it be too homely to refer to this position as a "product sales manager"? Similarly, would it not be preferable to refer to the executive in charge of selling to the school market as a "market manager" since he was "charged with the broad responsibility of securing more business in this field"?[37] Ames' reference to a product manager whose role was limited to keeping sales statistics and performing clerical tasks sounds very much like a "sales department staff assistant."[38]

While it is often correct to refer to a product manager as a marketing manager for a product, frequently his responsibilities are so broad that he is, in effect, the general manager of a "company."

> Companies have adopted the product division approach, centering, in effect, the general management of a "company within a company" on the shoulders of the product manager. He is generally given complete authority to the full extent of his responsibilities and is held accountable for the profit of his division.[39]

In instances such as the one illustrated, the title would more appropriately be "Marketing Manager-Product Division" or "Product Division Manager." (Since the authors had previously referred to the head of product divisions at General Foods, it is assumed that the manager is in charge of several related products. If only one product were in a division, the terms "product manager" and "division manager" could be used interchangeably. Although this situation would seldom occur, the status impli-

cation of the two terms would probably make "division manager" more desirable.)

The *Printers' Ink* product manager who "is interested in developing a broad line of products for use in his markets"[40] is not a true product manager because of his "broad line of products" and his market orientation. He is probably a divisional market manager. Again, the reference to a product manager with 203 products[41] probably refers to a division manager (the article does not indicate if he is a complete marketing manager or is oriented toward a single market).

From this discussion, it is possible to segregate the positions described in the section, "What is a product manager?" into the following titles:

1 Division manager—The executive who has the authority and responsibility to manage (or as Buskirk would say, "plan, direct, and control"[42]) the life cycle of a group of related products. (See Figures 4-3 and 4-4.)
2 Marketing manager—The executive who has the authority and responsibility to manage all the marketing activities for the products in a company or division. (See Figures 4-3 and 4-4.) In cases where the so-called "marketing concept" is employed, it is common for this official to have line authority over marketing activities and considerable functional authority over production and finance.

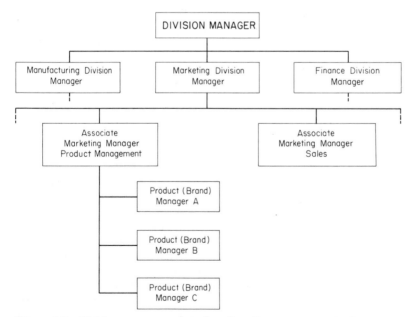

Figure 4-3   Division manager and product/brand manager organization.

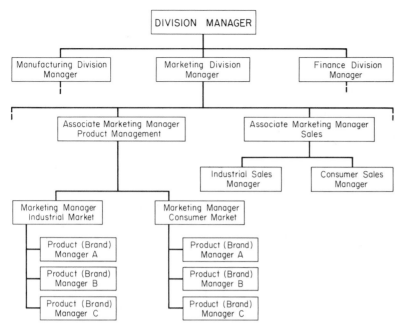

Figure 4-4   Division manager, market manager, and market product manager organization.

3 **Product manager**—The previously mentioned Schiff and Mellman definition should be refined as follows: the executive with primary authority and responsibility for the planning, direction, and control of all phases of a product's current existence. (See Figure 4-3.) This definition does not imply that the product manager has final or unrestricted authority or responsibility for all aspects of a product's life. Under the "marketing concept," however, functional authority belonging to the .marketing manager is often delegated to the individual product managers for their products and is, of course, subject to review by the marketing manager.

4 **Market product manager**—This position occurs when "the market manager may be so specialized that he devotes his attention to a single product for a single market."[43] This, however, is unusual. (See Figure 4-4.)

5 **Brand manager**—In most instances today, products are not sold but brands.[44] When purchases of products are made on the basis of brand preference, it is more accurate to refer to the executive responsible for managing the life cycle of the item as a brand manager. This is particularly true when one company markets competing brands within one product category. (See Figure 4-3.)

6 **Product specialist**—Unquestionably, there are instances where a staff position can be a valid way to insure individual attention and

interest for each product in a company's line without creating the problems of company-wide coordination which the delegation of extensive functional authority may require. If an individual has only the authority to suggest the marketing program for his product and then must negotiate with the other areas of the company for services to implement these plans, he does not possess a manager's ability to take decisive action and should not be called a product or brand manager. Rather, it seems that the contributions which such a position can offer in some situations could be made with equal effectiveness (and less confusion) if it were recognized as a different variety and called "product specialist."

GUIDELINES

Product management: still no panacea. Without doubt, the practice of product management is replete with potential pitfalls for the unskilled practitioner. The problem of the concept's scope has particularly manifested itself in the areas of authority, responsibility, and definition. A universal answer to the initial question of how much and what kind of authority the product manager should have can still not be given. A safe generalization, however, would be that sufficient authority must be granted to achieve the requirements of the position. A product or brand specialist with only staff authority lacks the quick, decisive power to act which can make the most effective use of his specialized knowledge and interest. Considerable functional authority is often given to the product manager because of his importance as a coordinating influence and because of the need to equate authority and responsibility. In order to avoid, or at least to minimize, conflict, functional authority thus delegated should be subject to over-all coordination one or, at the most, two levels immediately above the product manager.

Obviously, authority cannot be delegated, employees cannot be properly selected or trained, performance cannot be evaluated, and responsibility cannot be exacted until there is agreement on the meaning and scope of the position involved. An attempt has been made to evolve reasonable guidelines for classification of positions in the product management phylum. Operative definitions have been suggested as a means of revealing distinctions in the areas of activity and in the performance expected from various types of product-oriented organizations. Clarity is frequently a function of adequate understanding, and understanding begins with definition. This emphasis on semantics was aptly worded by Confucius: "If names be not used correctly, then speech gets tied up in knots; and if speech be so, then business comes to a standstill."[45]

References

1. "Why Modern Marketing Needs the Product Manager," *Printers' Ink*, CCLXXII (Oct. 4, 1960), 25.

2. Robert W. Lear, "No Easy Road to Market Orientation," *Harvard Business Review*, XLI (Sept.-Oct. 1963), 58.

3. R. H. Jacobs, "The Effective Use of the Product Manager," American Management Association, Marketing Series No. 97, 196, p. 31.

4. B. Charles Ames, "Pay Off From Product Management," *Harvard Business Review*, XLI (Nov.-Dec., 1963), 142.

5. Michael Schiff and Martin Mellman, *Financial Management of the Marketing Function* (New York: Financial Executives Research Foundation, Inc., 1962), pp. 28–29.

6. "What Makes P & G so Successful," *Printers' Ink*, CCLXXX (Sept. 28, 1962), 31.

7. Letter of Dec. 9, 1963, from C. C. Uhling, Manager, Public Relations Department, Procter and Gamble Company.

8. Procter & Gamble, "Intra-Company Product Competition," *Problems in Marketing, No. 2*, Students' Material, 1956, p. 1. Also see Alfred Lief, *It Floats* (New York: Rinehart & Co., 1958), p. 181.

9. Lief, *ibid.*, p. 182.

10. "Product Management: What Does It Mean?" *Sales Management*, April 17, 1959, p. 42.

11. Robert J. Kieth, "The Marketing Revolution," *Journal of Marketing*, XXIV (Jan. 1960), 35.

12. *Printers' Ink*, Oct. 14, 1960, *op. cit.*, p. 26.

13. "Career Opportunities with Colgate-Palmolive Company," a recruiting brochure, p. 4.

14. "Opportunities in Advertising," *What Now?* a Procter & Gamble recruiting brochure, p. 10.

15. R. H. Jacobs, *op. cit.*, p. 16.

16. L. P. Bucklin, "Organizing the Marketing Function in a Growth Industry," *California Management Review*, IV:2 (Winter 1962), 45.

17. Ames, *op. cit.*, p. 141.

18. F. F. Mauser, *Modern Marketing Management* (New York: McGraw-Hill Book Co., 1961), p. 57.

19. R. H. Buskirk, *Principles of Marketing* (New York: Holt, Rinehart, and Winston, Inc., 1961), p. 623.

20. *Ibid.*

21. See Lyndall F. Urwick, "The Problems of Management Semantics," *California Management Review*, II:3 (Spring 1960).

22. E. R. Weger, *Die Absatzwirtschaft*, March 1963, pp. 131–134.

23. W. K. A. Disch, "Review of *Die Absatzwirtschaft*," *Journal of Marketing*, XXVII (Oct. 1963), 116.

24. Schiff and Mellman, *op. cit.*, p. 246.

25. Ames, *op. cit.*, p. 142.

26. Jacobs, *op. cit.*, p. 16.

27. Bucklin, *op. cit.*

28. *Printers' Ink*, Oct. 14, 1960, *op. cit.*, p. 27.

29. *Ibid.*

30. Edward C. Bursk, *Text and Cases in Marketing* (Englewood Cliffs, N.J.: Prentice-Hall, Inc., 1962), p. 499.

31. H. W. Hepner, *Modern Marketing* (New York: McGraw-Hill Book Co., 1955), p. 448.

32. Based on Harold D. Koontz and Cyril O'Donnell, *Principles of Management* (New York: McGraw-Hill Book Co., 1964), p. 272.

33. *Ibid.*, p. 63.

34. J. S. Baumgartner, *Project Management* (Homewood, Ill.: Richard D. Irwin, Inc., 1963), p. 112.

35. *Ibid.*, p. 6. Figure 4-1 is also adapted from this source.

36. Mauser, *op. cit.*, p. 57.

37. Jacobs, *op. cit.*, p. 20.

38. Ames, *op. cit.*, p. 141.

39. H. Lazo and A. Corbin, *Management in Marketing* (New York: McGraw-Hill Book Co., 1961), p. 81.

40. *Printers' Ink,* Oct. 14, 1960, *op. cit.*, p. 27.

41. *Ibid.*, p. 30.

42. Buskirk, *op. cit.*, p. 623.

43. Lear, *op. cit.*, p. 58.

44. See B. Gardner and S. J. Levy, "The Product and The Brand," *Harvard Business Review,* LIII (March-April 1955), 33–39.

45. Quoted by Lyndall F. Urwick, *op. cit.*

READING 5

TOMORROW'S MANAGEMENT: A MORE ADVENTUROUS LIFE IN A FREE-FORM CORPORATION*

Max Ways

What industrialization was to the nineteenth century, management is to the twentieth. Almost unrecognized in 1900, management has become the central activity of our civilization. It employs a high proportion of our educated men and determines the pace and quality of our economic progress, the effectiveness of our government services, and the strength of our national defense. The way we "manage," the way we shape our organizations, affects and reflects what our society is becoming.

The essential task of modern management is to deal with change. Management is the agency through which most changes enter our society, and it is the agency that then must cope with the environment it has set in turbulent motion. To carry out its active social role of adaptation, management itself, therefore, must be adaptable. Already the nature of management has undergone drastic alterations. As it stands today on the threshold of the final

third of its first century, modern management seems pregnant with another metamorphosis. It is now possible to see in outline the shapes toward which the next generation of management will tend.

One of the more obvious questions of the last ten years has been whether the number of management men will continue to expand faster than the economy. Will many of the millions now pouring forth from the universities find that management is a contracting job market in which they will be surplus? The question is currently linked with predictions about the computer revolution. Without doubt, computers have taken over some work formerly done by middle management, and are capable of taking over much more. But this fact is only a part of the whole busy scene. Management is still expanding and probably will continue to expand as new tasks are created. Indeed, the new information technology represented by computers is one of the important factors creating the new tasks.

A less obvious question raised by the com-

* Reprinted with permission of Fortune Magazine, July 1, 1966.

puters bears on the character, rather than the size, of future management. Will instant access by top management to operational information reverse the trend toward managerial decentralization, which has had the salutary effect of giving more independent scope to more people? It is easy to think of examples where authority now dispersed might be efficiently reconcentrated at the top with the aid of computers. But such reconcentration is not the main trend in organization today. Since the new information technology began coming into use in the Fifties, the trend toward decentralization has probably been accelerated, indicating that there were better reasons for decentralization than the lack of instant information at headquarters. Computers can be used to reinforce either a centralizing policy or its opposite; the probability increases that decentralization will in the coming decades be carried to lengths undreamed of ten years ago.

Much more is involved in these issues than the relative short-run efficiency of men and computers. One can even accept the prediction that the computer revolution will prove to be a more important development than the industrial revolution, and yet see both industrialization and computerization as details in the still broader sweep of a historical era wherein men for the first time deliberately organized their civilization around the processes of social change. In this larger context, both practitioners of management and academic observers of it are developing radically new ideas about what it should and will become. Some of these projections are the more surprising because modern management, in its brief history, has been widely misunderstood. Actual management is already decades ahead of the popular myths about how it works.

THE STAND-INS FOR MR. LEGREE

Assets, they say, make men conservative. Because language, incomparably the greatest in mankind's social assets, changes slowly, we are forced to describe the new and unfamiliar in terms drawn from the old and familiar. Since some change occurs in any period there is always a lag between actuality and the past-bound words we use to describe it. Where change is slow or is confined to a narrow segment of life, this language lag does no great harm. In the fast-changing twentieth century,

however, the language lag causes untold confusion.

Corporations, government agencies, and scientific institutes are really quite different from tribes, families, armies, feudal estates, and monasteries, but our ideas of the newer organizations are distorted by an anachronistic vocabulary drawn from the older group. Business leaders of the late nineteenth century were called "captains of industry" or "robber barons." Government bureaus have "chief." Many present-day organizations still think they operate by "chains of command." From one point of view, management stands in the place of "the owner," a historically familiar figure; it is easy to slip into the habit of talking about a company as if it were merely a complicated kind of plantation with hundreds of "overseers" substituted for Mr. Legree.

As late as the 1920's some American law schools were handling what little they had to say about the internal life of corporations under the rubric of "the law of master and servant." The very word "manager" suggests— even more strongly than "management"—that the basis of the activity is power over other men. (In the 1950's General Electric recognized that a large proportion of the people in management did not, in any literal sense, "manage." G.E. began to speak of management as made up of two groups: managers and "functional individual contributors." The number of "fics," who may be physical or social scientists, lawyers or public-relations experts and who are often future managers or ex-managers, is increasing in nearly all large companies.) In short, the early image of the corporation was heavily loaded on the side of authoritarianism because the early vocabulary pertaining to management came from the patriarchal family, from military organization, from legal concepts of ownership, and from memories of the feudal hierarchy.

Upon this primal image of the corporation some less antique but equally misleading concepts were then superimposed. The science of economics developed in the nineteenth century when the public had become familiar with mechanical principles. Both classical and Marxist economics leaned heavily on mechanical analogies. The economists' model still in service today is a machine. Since humanity is that element in economics least susceptible to mechanical treatment and prediction, economics tends to suppress the human factors. "Economic man" is the most oversimplified of all views of our otherwise interesting species. Man's astounding capacities must be expressed in erglike units, man's even more astounding appetites must be reduced to chilly abstractions resembling Newton's gravitational pull, and man's most profound uncertainties must be ignored because they cannot be quantified. This dehumanized economists' model of the total economy, recast in compact form, merged with the older authoritarian myth of the corporation. The resulting popular image: a kind of life-with-father, automated.

BUREAUCRACY AS A MACHINE

Early in the twentieth century the great German sociologist Max Weber, noting common elements in business organization, government bureaus, and the Prussian military structure, called the new organizational form "bureaucracy." In a bureaucratic system, public or private business was carried out "according to *calculable rules* and 'without regard for persons.'" Functionaries with specialized training learn their tasks better by practice. "Precision, speed, unambiguity . . . unity, strict subordination, reduction of friction—these are raised to the optimum point in the strictly bureaucratic administration, and especially in its monocratic form." Weber said the new form was succeeding because the "bureaucratic mechanism compares with other organizations exactly as does the machine with the non-mechanical modes of production." Around the same time, Frederick W. Taylor in the U.S. promulgated "scientific management" in which workers were regarded as parts of a corporate machine, the excellence of which was to be measured, of course, by its "efficiency."

It is against this persistent image of dehumanized modern organization that students today react with the sort of castration phobia expressed in the picket-sign slogan: "I am a human being; do not fold, bend, or mutilate." This fear and defiance of modern organization appears in scores of novels and plays, which restate Charlie Chaplin's *Modern Times;* the myth is the root of many anti-business (and some anti-government) attitudes; it even pervades management itself, souring fruitful careers with the sense that life is being sacrificed to a domineering and impersonal organization. The man who says, "I am a cog" does not

thereby become a cog—but he may become an unhappy and "alienated" man.

BEYOND EFFICIENCY LIE THE HUMAN QUALITIES

Whatever of truth there once was in the myth of the modern organization as a tyrannical machine has been diminishing for fifty years. The myth never took account of the modern organization's essential involvement in change. As this involvement has deepened, reality and myth have drifted further apart. Around 1900 there was many a one-product manufacturer with a stable technology and a well-defined, reliable market. Such a company could increase its efficiency by routinizing more and more of its decisions into what Max Weber had called "calculable rules." Companies in this situation are exceedingly rare today. In the Sixties, a typical company makes scores, perhaps hundreds or thousands, of products, which it knows it will soon have to abandon or drastically modify; it must substitute others selected from millions of possibilities. Most of the actual and possible products are affected by rapidly changing techniques of production and distribution. Present and prospective markets are enticingly expansive, but fiercely competitive, loosely defined, and unstable.

In this situation, a company cannot be rigidly designed, like a machine, around a fixed goal. A smaller proportion of decisions can be routinized or precoded for future use. The highest activity of management becomes a continuous process of decision about the nature of the business. Management's degree of excellence is still judged in part by its efficiency of operation, but much more by its ability to make decisions changing its product mix, its markets, its techniques of financing and selling. Initiative, flexibility, creativity, adaptability are the qualities now required—and these are far more "human" than the old mechanical desideratum, efficiency.

The institutional system of the Soviet Union has been rigidly organized on the old bureaucratic model. Central authority fixes a definite goal, whether an increase in steel production or a vehicle to reach the moon. Material and human resources are mobilized around that goal. In terms of sheer efficiency certain aspects of the Soviet system work well. Yet we are right in regarding the U.S.S.R. as a "backward" country, and certain Russian leaders are justified in their recent efforts to move toward a more flexible and decentralized system. To cope with a very fluid technological and social environment such as that of the U.S., Soviet management would need much greater emphasis on the specifically human qualities.

Even U.S. governmental institutions, which are years behind our corporations in the evolution of management, are now using flexible approaches inconceivable in the U.S.S.R. The U.S. has consciously embarked on a huge effort to improve the quality of education without defining in any but the vaguest terms what that "improved" quality might be. We assume that through a highly decentralized educational system we may be able to grope our way "forward," step by step, forming new values and new targets as we proceed from choice to choice. In a similar spirit, we have begun an effort to improve the Appalachian region without knowing in advance what we want Appalachia to become. We have no centrally designed plan for Appalachia, but we believe that if the effort is "well managed," in the new (nonbureaucratic) sense of that phrase, a livelier Appalachia may result from the federal government's stimulation of changeful decisions by individuals, communities, and organizations in Appalachia. It is impossible to imagine the U.S.S.R.—or any other organization formed along the old authoritarian, machine-like lines —generating organized activity without first defining "the task."

MANAGEMENT AND CHANGE NEED EACH OTHER

U.S. corporations are pioneering the movement toward the new style of management because they are more heavily engaged than any other category of organization on the frontiers of actual social innovation. It is true, of course, that the main base of modern innovation lies in scientific discovery, most of which is—and all of which could be—carried on independently of business organizations. But the mission of science is to discover new truth; it is not organized to perform the additional and very different work of transforming discoveries into technological inventions; still less is it organized for the third stage of introducing these

inventions into actual use. Usually, scientific discovery is the product of concentrated specialization in a field of study. Innovation, on the contrary, almost always requires various kinds of specialized knowledge drawn from many fields. One of the primary functions of modern management is to assemble various skills and coordinate them in production.

Science and technology, which make possible an ever increasing range of products and services, do not tell us which of these to produce. So another task of management is to mediate between the evolving wants of society and the evolving abilities for satisfying those wants. This mission, performed within a competitive market system, also requires many kinds of specialized knowledge—e.g., market research, cost analysis—and very complex and delicate coordination. The whole process is suffused—as science is not—with questions of *value*, questions of whether the corporation and its customers want A rather than B. The judgments of management are relative and they are often intuitive—i.e., based upon incomplete and perhaps unreliable information. Management's hunger for knowledge on which to base decisions becomes ever stronger, but is fated to be forever unsatisfied. The advance of knowledge does not reduce the remaining body of ignorance because "possible knowledge" is not a finite quantity. In practical affairs, as in science, the more we learn the more questions confront us. Innovation does not wait until risk of failure has been eliminated by complete knowledge; in an era of radical change, management cannot be designed to work like a machine on the assumption that the goals and conditions that determined its design will remain constant.

Although statistical comparisons are impossible, it is almost certainly true that the numbers employed in "management" have been growing more rapidly than the total economy during the past fifty years. If we apply the old bureaucratic machine standards of efficiency we are led to suppose that the vast increase in the numbers of management men represents the wasteful working of Parkinson's Law. But if the prime mission of management is to deal with change, then the size of management should be roughly proportionate to the rate of innovation rather than to the amount of physical output. This explains why the U.S. needs a proportionately larger managerial force than the less lively economy of the U.S.S.R. For years it has been obvious that in numbers and in quality British management was inferior to that of the U.S. and that Britain was not educating nearly enough men to fill its assumed management need. Yet no acute British "shortage" of management personnel exists in the sense that the market there places a very high price in money or prestige on management men; in fact, during the past twenty years a high proportion of men with the kind of training regarded as needed in management have emigrated from Britain, feeling their abilities to be in surplus in a relatively stagnant society. To take a more extreme example, the African nation of Gambia, which produces very few managerial types, would be the world's worst place to look for a job in management.

It appears that the need for management cannot be calculated on a simple supply-and-demand basis, because management creates change and change creates the need for management. As the "inventory" of management people in a society rises (in quantity and quality) the demand for still more management rises with it; or, to put in another way, the rate of innovation and the managerial function are interdependent. Except on a short-range basis or in respect to specific categories of management work, it is pointless to talk about a "shortage" or a "surplus" of managers.

Seen in this perspective, the computer revolution, by powerfully enhancing management's effectiveness in dealing with change, should have the long-range effect of increasing demand for management men. U.S. experience to date seems to support this theoretical expectation. Recruiting for management (of both managers, strictly so-called, and of such "functional individual contributors" as scientists, engineers, accountants) has never been more active, as any reader of newspaper advertisements is aware. More significantly, corporations are making increasing efforts to identify early the men with a high management potential, to train them rapidly, and to promote them to jobs of greater responsibility. This tendency seems especially marked in companies that have been quick to make use of computers. Probably the new information technology has had the effect of breaking bottlenecks that had restrained these companies from generating innovation and coping with the changing environment.

BACK TO THE FAMILY FIRM?

Not everyone expected this expansion of management. In 1958, when the computer revolution was young, two respected observers of management, Harold J. Leavitt and Thomas L. Whisler, wrote for the *Harvard Business Review* a much-discussed article entitled "Management in the 1980's." The article made a persuasive case for the proposition that the new information technology would reverse the trend toward decentralized and "participative" management. Leavitt and Whisler said: "In one respect, the picture we might paint for the 1980's bears a strong resemblance to the organizations of certain other societies—e.g., to the family dominated organizations of Italy and other parts of Europe, and even to a small number of such firms in our own country. There will be many fewer middle managers, and most of those who remain are likely to be routine technicians rather than thinkers." At the end came this portentous note: "We may have to reappraise our traditional notions about the worth of the individual as opposed to the organization."

Seven years later, with much more evidence to draw upon, H. Igor Ansoff, professor of industrial administration at Carnegie Institute of Technology, wrote for the *Harvard Business Review* a sort of answer to Leavitt and Whisler. In "The Firm of the Future," Ansoff said that the right question was not what the new information technology would do to management but "how will the manager use these extraordinarily powerful tools in furthering the objectives of the firm in its environment of the future." Since "the forces which will shape the future firm are already at work ... the shape of the firm in the 1980's ... need not be perceived dimly through a crystal ball [but] can be sketched by analyzing and projecting from the present." He listed three trends in the business environment: (1) *product dynamics*—"the life cycles of products will become shorter"; (2) *market dynamics*—"as superior technology displaces it from its traditional markets, the firm has to fight back by looking for new pastures" and the growing internationalization of markets will add to the competitive "turbulence"; (3) *firm and society*—governmental and social limits on the firm's behavior will increase so that "its search for profit will be strongly affected by an awareness of social consequences." The firm of the future would be able to program many of its activities, thus releasing management to deal with the increasing load of "non-programmable" decisions that would confront it in the new environment.

The manager to match these formidable new conditions would be "broader gauged than his present counterpart." He would need a grip on the firm's technology, but he would also have to deal with problems on "a combined economic-political-cultural level." The new environment would call for more managerial skill in human relations. "Increasing importance will be placed on the manager's ability to communicate rapidly and intelligibly, gain acceptance for change and innovation, and motivate and lead people in new and varying directions." Ansoff was not worried that management might be made obsolescent by new information technology. "The manager of the future will need all the computer help that he can get in coping with the greatly increased complexity of his job."

"MAN IS A WANTING ANIMAL"

The fluid business environment of the future will demand not only a different kind of manager but a different organizational structure. Management's need to keep redefining "the nature of the business" applies not only to the product mix but also to the internal arrangements of the organization. One reason why men and their organizations may fail to adapt is that they cling to erroneous ideas about themselves and/or their situation. The late Douglas M. McGregor, of the Sloan School of Management of M.I.T., believed that the evolution of organizations was being retarded by a set of erroneous beliefs about man and his work which he called Theory X. The average man dislikes work, according to Theory X, and must therefore be coerced, directed, and controlled. He can be made to contribute to the achievement of organizational objectives only by a threat to the supply of his physiological needs. He seeks security and wishes to avoid responsibility for decisions. The old idea of authoritarian, paternalistic organizations fits Theory X; it is better for all concerned if power can be concentrated in the exceptional men at the top, who like responsibility.

Today men respond to certain stimuli that McGregor wrapped in a proposition called Theory Y. They take for granted the fulfillment of their basic material needs. "A satisfied need," McGregor said, "is not a motivator of behavior. Man is a wanting animal, [and his] needs are organized in a series of levels—a hierarchy of importance." A man whose stomach is satisfied by a secure supply becomes conscious of needs at a higher level. He seeks to feed his ego, which is more insatiable than any stomach, and to achieve a richer sense of his own identity. Many of these higher wants can best be satisfied by the kind of work that has a substantial content of intellectual activity and moral choice. Our society is by no means affluent in providing work of this sort, but more and more men in the professional and managerial category are finding their highest rewards in responsible work itself rather than merely in their pay.

Obviously, an organization based on the assumptions of Theory Y will array itself very differently from the old pyramid, where as much authority as possible was concentrated at the top. A Theory Y corporation would *prefer* to distribute responsibility widely among its managers, even if decision making could be centralized without loss of efficiency. A Theory X organization wants each individual to perform reliably the function assigned to him in the design of the total machine; a Theory Y organization wants an individual to be involved consciously in the relations between what he does and what others are doing; it wants him to seek ways of improving those relations in terms of his own expanding goals and the changing goals of the organization; it wants the individual to participate in setting goals for himself and for the organization.

FAREWELL TO FAUST

What McGregor did was to put a solider and more "human" base under older theories of "participative" management, which had slopped over into the dubious proposition (derisively referred to as "the contented-cow psychology") that the way to make workers efficient was to make them happy. McGregor's Theory Y allows plenty of room for discontent and tension; it provides, however, a realistic way to reconcile the needs of the individual with the objectives of the organization. The individual is no longer seen as entering a corrupt Faustian barter in which he abandons his "soul" in ex-

change for material satisfactions and power—
a deal that will become increasingly repugnant
to the more highly educated men that management will require. In short, the kind of management called for by Ansoff's projection of the
future business environment could be provided
under Theory Y much better than under Theory X.

Warren G. Bennis, McGregor's successor as
chairman of the Organization Studies Group
at M.I.T., asserts in a recent book, *Changing
Organizations,* that during the past decade "the
basic philosophy which underlies managerial
behavior" has made a fundamental shift in the
direction of Theory Y. Bennis discerns the
philosophic shift in three areas:

> 1 A new concept of man, based on in-
> creased knowledge of his complex and
> shifting needs, which replaces the over-
> simplified, innocent push-button idea of
> man.
> 2 A new concept of power, based on col-
> laboration and reason, which replaces a
> model of power based on coercion and
> fear.
> 3 A new concept of organization values,
> based on humanistic-democratic ideals,
> which replaces the depersonalized mech-
> anistic value system of bureaucracy.

Bennis is quick to say he does not mean that
these transformations "are fully accepted or
even understood, to say nothing of imple-
mented in day-to-day affairs." But, "they have
gained wide intellectual acceptance in enlight-
ened management quarters . . . have caused a
tremendous amount of rethinking on the part
of many organizations, and . . . have been used
as a basis for policy formulation by many large-
scale organizations." The shift in philosophy
and the practical predicaments arising out of
twentieth-century changes in the environment
support one another in encouraging management to accelerate its own evolution. Business
organizations, Bennis believes, are leading the
way in replacing the old "bureaucratic mechanism," which was "capable of coordinating
men and power in a stable society of routine
tasks [but] cannot cope with contemporary
realities."

ASSETS NOT ON THE BALANCE SHEET

The business scene of 1966 shows substantial
evidence to support this view. Some of the evi-

dence lies in what business leaders are saying,
and some in what they are doing. One significant change is the increasing sense that management is the chief asset of the corporation
rather than an overhead expense. "Investment
for modernizing plant and equipment is often
wasted unless there is a corresponding investment in the managerial and technical talent
to run it," says M. J. Rathbone, former board
chairman of Standard Oil (New Jersey). He
notes that the valuation of a corporation's se-
curities is based more upon appraisals of the
quality of its management than upon the
corporation's inanimate assets.

Many advanced companies engage in "total
career development," a conscious policy of
maximizing managerial quality over the long
run by balancing the old criterion of finding
the best man for the job with some consideration of the best job for the development of the
man. This policy is pursued even where it results in some short-run sacrifice of efficiency.
Sears, Roebuck has for many years carried on
an elaborate effort to identify as early as possible those individuals who have a high potential
for development, and to measure as accurately
as possible how they respond to various kinds
of managerial challenges. Polaroid has taken a
further step in the Theory Y direction; instead
of having its top management planning the
paths for executive careers, Polaroid uses a
"posting system" in which its men are encour-
aged to compete for forthcoming job vacancies.
General Electric's intense concern with the development of managers includes the belief that
the man himself sets the objectives for his career and that the company must make an organized effort to keep open the means by
which an individual can broaden his responsibilities, along lines he chooses himself.

The concern for broadening responsibilities
goes all the way down to men recently recruited from college. Companies have noted
with alarm that many young people, recruited
after considerable effort, quit in the first year
or two. The pay may be satisfactory, but they
complain that their jobs are "too routine," or
"not demanding enough." To meet this criticism, some companies are giving trainees jobs
in which they can make costly mistakes. "There
is no justification left for prolonged training
procedures that prevent people from taking
responsibility," says Frederick R. Kappel, chairman of A.T.&T. "There is no excuse for the
timid doling out of oversupervised little jobs

that allow a person no opportunity to show what he can do." Noting that many youngsters find business goals "too narrow" to fire their imaginations, Kappel counters with a broad one: In the "interaction of science and society," he says, "it is the goal of business management to translate discovery into use. Our job in industry is to assimilate the scientific revolution in such a way that practical values will flow to the public, to society at large, in the most orderly and economical way."

THE WHITE SPACE BETWEEN THE BOXES

The structure of science is loose-jointed, non-pyramidal, non-authoritarian. The same adjectives apply to the structure of modern "society at large." Working between science and society, two fluid and unpredictable worlds, corporations must not let their own structures petrify.

Companies alert to the danger, therefore, have set up continuous reviews of their organization charts. At least one company goes so far as to engage in periodic shake-ups, just to keep its structure from "freezing." A more intelligent way is represented by those companies (including U.S. Rubber and Kimberly-Clark) that have set up permanent analytical staffs to find out how parts of the company actually relate and figure out how they ought to relate. In the search for more flexible structures the old distinctions between staff and line and the old walls between specialists and between departments tend to blur. "The interesting part of the organization chart," says one management consultant, "is in the white space between the boxes. That's where the real activity goes on."

The organizations now evolving on the beliefs of Theory Y represent a shift from a mechanical to an organic model that confronts managers with more subtle and complex challenges. How, for instance, is the unity and coherence of the organization to be maintained in an evolving free-form structure of mobile individuals?

Transitionally, a lot of authority is still concentrated at "the top," but it exists as a reserve to deal with crisis, major internal conflict, and the fundamental decisions affecting the whole organization that cannot, under present conceptions, be made elsewhere. Some management analysts, searching for the shape of the future, are looking intently at large, diversified corporations whose divisions and subdivisions are now competing actively against one another within a loose corporate framework. Can this internal competition be stepped up by rewriting the rules of the game and improving the scoring system? If "the market" is a good way to organize the economy as a whole, why not deliberately make the corporation's internal structure more market-like? At present, the resources of the firm tend to flow toward those divisions where the return on investment has been highest; this "rule" may put too much emphasis on the past. Accountancy, concentrating on the record of what has happened, has not paid enough attention to projecting comparisons between the probable future prospects of several divisions of a company. The Defense Department's work in projecting the comparative cost effectiveness of different weapon systems not yet in being has given business a powerful impetus in the direction of a new kind of accountancy oriented toward the future. Computers, by simulating the results and costs of competing projects, can be of immense help in this kind of accountancy.

Thinking along the lines of an internal corporate market, Professor Jay Forrester of M.I.T. wants companies to get rid of the familiar budget centers, replacing them with profit centers. The budget-center system sets up a conflict between those groups (production, sales, research, etc.) whose interest is to spend and those groups whose function is to restrain spending, such as the controller's office. Because such conflicts can be resolved only at the top of the corporation, the budget-center system perpetuates the authoritarian form of organization. Internal profit centers, on the contrary, demand self-restraint because no group has an interest in spending, as such, or in saving, as such. Every group has an interest in the difference between them—i.e., profit.

Forrester would also break up such central services as purchasing and drafting rooms. Created in the name of efficiency, they can result in "internal monopolies" that tend to become somnolent and unresponsive to the need for change. Moreover, they confuse the accounting system within which internal competition is conducted. The economies of scale that they are supposed to produce are not worth what they cost in deadening the initiative and responsiveness of the corporation.

THE INDEPENDENT PROFESSIONALS

The substitution of structures in which more people exercise self-control fits with the broadest trends in modern society. Professor Bennis believes that "democracy is inevitable" because it "is the only system which can successfully cope with the changing demands of contemporary civilization." By democracy, Bennis means "a climate of beliefs" including "full and free communication, regardless of rank and power; a reliance on consensus, rather than . . . coercion or compromise, to manage conflict; the idea that influence is based on technical competence and knowledge rather than on the vagaries of personal whims or prerogatives of power; [and] a basically human bias, one which accepts the inevitability of conflict between the organization and the individual but which is willing to cope with and mediate this conflict on rational grounds."

Not everybody would use the word democracy to describe this set of beliefs, but the contrast between this "climate" and that of the authoritarian machine-like organization is clear. It is also clear that the actual trends in U.S. management are moving in this direction and not back toward the shape forecast by Leavitt and Whisler, "the family dominated organizations of Italy and other parts of Europe."

"Professionalism" is here to stay a while. The scientist, engineer, and lawyer are indispensable to management and so are "professional" communicators and others whose skill lies in the coordination and leadership of specialists. The professional man in management has a powerful base of independence—perhaps a firmer base than the small businessman ever had in his property rights. The highly trained young man entering management today can look for corporate aid in enhancing his competence and hence his base of independence. He need not aspire to becoming *the* top officer of the firm, who holds the only "human" job in an organization conceived on the old line of a machine with all its decision-making initiative concentrated in the "operator" at the top. Today's management recruit can—and, in fact, does—have the more rational and less frustrating ambition of a life of ever widening responsibility and choices. The prospect for a managerial career today is more adventurous than it ever was, because by the year 2000 there will be hundreds of thousands, perhaps millions, of Americans, whose influence on the quality of life in their more fluid society will be greater than that of any past "captain of industry."

SECTION 2

Systems Concepts and Applications

The systems concept is much more widely discussed than understood. Probably no concept has ever had more lip service paid to it; undoubtedly few concepts have ever been more widely applied by people who did not know that they were doing so, and perhaps no concept has been more widely ignored by people who should know better.

Virtually anything except the simplest organism can be considered to be a system. The universe is the most general system of which we are all a part. Each system may be made up of subsystems, and in turn, each subsystem can itself be composed of sub-subsystems.

The "systems approach" involves the elementary idea that a system is composed of many interrelated parts; primary concern should therefore be given to the overall effectiveness of the system (rather than to the effectiveness of the respective subsystems) and to the interdependencies of the elements of the system. Of course, this idea is applicable at any organizational level. The marketing department is a system composed of subsystems and the business enterprise is a system of which marketing is a subsystem. In applying systems concepts to such an organization, overall corporate objectives and performance measures need be considered, rather than merely giving consideration to the parochial objectives of the subsystems, e.g., marketing, production, or finance. This may produce an overall result which is distinctly nonoptimal for a subsystem. For example, the corporate decision may be taken that short production runs of many products should be made so that a wide variety of different *items will be in stock for sale. The apparent performance of the production department will suffer, since through short runs, they will incur high costs. But, if more sales are produced, the overall net result to the company may be positive.*

This Section provides both basic systems concepts and applications of systems ideas in a variety of areas. The emphasis is a pragmatic one since the editors feel that it is at this level that the greatest payoffs are to be gained.

The variety of levels, both conceptual and organizational, at which systems concepts have proved useful, deserves some further emphasis. There is no monopoly on systems ideas at the corporate level. The development of a weapons system requires a management system, for example. The "systems management techniques" (discussed by Morrison) of the Department of Defense serve to illustrate this diversity of levels and variety of system applications.

Taken together, these selections provide sound evidence on which to base a prediction that the use of system ideas will become of increasing significance in both the government and business sectors of our society.

READING 6

THE SYSTEMS CONCEPT *

E. W. Martin, Jr.

The concept of a "system" is getting a great deal of attention in both industrial and academic management circles. Unfortunately, the word has many meanings; for purposes of this discussion, a system is simply an assemblage or combination of things or parts forming a complex whole. One of its most important characteristics is that it is composed of a hierarchy of subsystems. That is, the parts that form the major system may themselves be systems, and their parts may be systems, and so on. For example, the world economy can be considered to be a system in which the various national economies are subsystems. In turn, each national economy is composed of its various industries; each industry is composed of firms; and, of course, a firm can be considered a system composed of subsystems such as production, marketing, finance, accounting, and so on.

The systems concept does not provide a set of rules for solving all problems, but it is a

* *Reprinted with permission from* Business Horizons, *Spring, 1966.*

useful device for viewing many phenomena. First, it assumes that a system can be understood and that it should be designed to accomplish its purpose. Furthermore, systems concepts emphasize the relationships between the parts and how these relationships affect the performance of the overall system. This viewpoint also allows us to apply knowledge concerning living organisms and complex electronic or mechanized systems to organizational systems. Living organisms are self-adaptive systems in the Darwinian sense; those organisms survive that are able to adapt successfully to their changing environment. Analogously, an organization that wants to be successful in the long run must be capable of adapting to a changing (and perhaps hostile) competitive environment. Perhaps a management task of a higher order is to design the organizational system so that it adapts successfully.

Practical men have long recognized difficulties involved in coping with complex systems, for it is difficult to foresee the consequences of changes in the parts. After making the changes necessary to install and effectively use an electronic computer, for example, many organizations have found that human reactions produce entirely unexpected consequences, which effectively nullify the desired changes.

When we attempt to understand complex systems, problems arise at two distinct levels: the micro level (understanding the basic cause-and-effect relationships governing the performances of the almost elementary subsystems) and the macro level (understanding the effect on systems performance of the complex chains of interrelationships between the elementary subsystems). Historically, we have been able to cope reasonably well with the micro problems by isolating them, studying them in some detail, and building models incorporating the relationships. On the other hand, we have failed miserably at the macro level, frequently by simply ignoring the existence of important relationships.

Some of our difficulties in attempting to educate people for management responsibilities are closely related to these macro systems problems. We can teach individual subjects, but the student frequently cannot integrate his knowledge to form an understanding of the total organization. This failure may occur because a modern business is extremely complex; it also occurs because the process of integration seems to require a high degree of intuition. Even those who do understand the macro aspects of the system do not really know how they do it, and as organizational systems become more complex, the problems of integration may tax the capacity of even the most advanced intuition.

Is there no solution to understanding the operation of complex systems other than through pure intuition or trial-and-error experimentation? One modern approach to problem solving is to build a mathematical model that incorporates the pertinent variables and their interrelationships into a set of equations that can be solved by a computer. Unfortunately, for any complex system, the number of variables and their intricate interrelationships make this approach impossible; the resulting mathematical problem usually can't be solved even by the most powerful computers. Conse-quently, the mathematical model although quite successful in coping with micro systems problems, has been inadequate in attacking over-all problems.

Fortunately, the combination of the viewpoint of an organization as a system, a model-building approach, and the utilization of powerful computers can be synthesized to produce a technique called systems simulation, which shows promise for analyzing and designing complex organization systems. In brief, a simulation model links individual mathematical models (representing the system's micro components or elementary subsystems) with the computer program (incorporating the macro aspects). The simulation model may be operated at a speed that compresses many years of real time into a small amount of computer time; thus a history of performance of the simulated systems under specified conditions can be obtained. The performance of the over-all system also can be observed under changes in conditions, changes in characteristics of the individual components, or changes in the interrelationships between the components.

It must be emphasized that the usefulness of systems simulation depends upon our ability to understand the micro components of the system and their basic interrelationships. This is not easy, for we simply do not have a detailed understanding of organizational systems. However, the construction of a model forces us to ask the right questions, and to begin to obtain understanding.

Thus we are led to a final concept of this discussion, that of organizational research and development. This long-range investment of resources (both money and talent) has the objective of understanding the organizational system and improving its performance. Like product R&D, this investment is risky in that it is impossible to predict the outcome with certainty. However, over the past twenty years our aggregate investment in product R&D has completely transformed our economy. It seems likely that long-range and continuous investment in organizational R&D will have a similar revolutionary impact through improved performance.

READING 7

ORGANIZATION AS A TOTAL SYSTEM *

Stanley Young

Increasingly, organizations are being considered from a systems point of view in both a descriptive and normative context.[1] Ashby's work would exemplify some of the descriptive work. System's Development Corporation, Strategic Air Command, and Lockheed are effectively using the systems concept to redesign major phases of organizations in an operational and normative sense.[2] Many companies have expended similar efforts to certain subsystems such as steel-rolling mills and oil refineries.[3]

What appears to be occurring is that our conception of the organization is changing from one of structure to one of process. Rather than visualize the organization in its traditional structural, bureaucratic, and hierarchical motif, with a fixed set of authority relationships much like the scaffolding of a building, we are beginning to view organization as a set of flows, information, men, material, and behavior. Time

and change are the critical aspects. This change in construct will become more pronounced in the future because (and this is an assertion which I will not attempt to defend) I believe the systems approach is more productive. If we consider organization from a normative point of view, there is another reason for this trend which is of more immediate concern and is the working hypothesis of this paper. Only when the organization is designed (Organizational Planning) from a systems orientation will it be able to take full advantage of the new and emerging managerial technologies which include quantitative methods, the computer, information sciences, and the behavioral sciences. Although I will not attempt to prove this proposition in the rigorous sense, the balance of this analysis will be directed toward demonstrating how this might be accomplished.

However, before taking up this thesis, let us note the problems which currently exist that hinder the effective utilization of managerial technology. One problem relates to the absence of a construct as to how the new technology is

* Reprinted from California Management Review, vol. X, no. 3, Spring, 1968. Copyright 1968 by The Regents of The University of California.

to be used in an integrated and systematic manner; or consider it as the absence of a meaningful gestalt or whole into which such a technology would logically fit. What does exist might be categorized as a tool chest or "bits and pieces" state.

For example, let us suppose that a personnel manager has what he believes is a problem —excessive absenteeism. Given the external and internal environment of the firm, the organizational constraints he has as a manager, and a set of behavioral information and managerial tools, how does he reduce the absenteeism rate? He knows something about psychology— perception, cognition, learning and motivation theory—social psychology, attitude formation, and resistance to change. From sociology he recalls group theory; he can calculate the median, mean and mode, run a correlation and find a derivative. In other words, he is a qualified MBA student. Specifically, what should he do to reduce the absenteeism rate? The students and practitioners are given a tool chest filled with bits and pieces: a little math, a little psychology, a little sociology, and the manager is then admonished to build a better house. How is the application of the technology to be integrated so that the manager can be relatively assured that he is achieving a desired result? What is missing is the bridge or discipline between tools and organizational results. That those of a more traditional bent remain somewhat skeptical of the newer managerial technology is understandable.

Although one can raise many serious questions as to the reality, validity, predictability, and effectiveness of the classical principles approach, nevertheless, it can be said that it roughly holds together as a whole or single unit, and its parts are related in a logical fashion. Starting with the concept of private property and the delegation of authority, the organizational chart is drawn; authority is allocated; a division of labor is specified; the functions of management are outlined and planning, organizing, and staffing are conducted. A certain internal logic is present, not unlike the economist's model of perfect competition. The parts are related to each other in a particular manner. Viewed as a single construct, and traditional model is understandable and operational to students and practitioners alike.

The same cannot be said for the newer managerial technology. The General Management or Organization Theorist's domain is the whole. One is concerned with the problem of organization space, or the distance between subfunctions, subprocesses, tools, and techniques—the interface problems. To those who are concerned with the whole, the "bits and pieces" approach of the new technology is disconcerting. Where and how do all these parts fit together and what is the relationship between one piece and another? Sprinkling behavioral and quantitative courses about a business curriculum is of questionable effectiveness and has not, I believe, changed the basic manner in which organizations are managed. Therefore, as far as the newer technologies are concerned, a gestalt or general model has been missing which will integrate all the bits and pieces meaningfully. I am suggesting that the systems approach will provide this model.

Another problem which has emerged requiring the organization to be designed as a total system, is that all too frequently the organizational context into which the newer technologies are placed tend to be inappropriate. We are attaching sophisticated techniques to a primitive vehicle, the bureaucratic structure. Organizations should be designed around the technology; technology should not be forced to fit an existing structure. Thus some corporations, to be fashionable, have created operations research departments which, in fact, have been given little or nothing to do. One case was reported in which the primary duty of the O.R. official was to solve the school math problems of the Corporate President's daughter.

In the history of innovation one frequently finds that when a new device is invented, it is attached to the existing model. For example, when the gasoline motor was first invented, it was connected to a buggy. However, as additional innovations occurred, the vehicle itself eventually had to be modified. If advantage was to be taken of additional improvements, obviously one could not unite a 300 horsepower motor to a light shay with wooden wheels and axles. If innovation follows its normal course, we can expect the new managerial techniques to force a modification in the traditional organizational arrangements. This, indeed, has been taking place. The exploitation of the computer, particularly when utilized in an on-line capacity, has led to a weakening or abolishment of the traditional divisional or departmental lines of authority. Improvements in